# The Ecology of Homicide

*Race, Place, and Space in Postwar Philadelphia*

Eric C. Schneider

**PENN**

UNIVERSITY OF PENNSYLVANIA PRESS

PHILADELPHIA

Published by
University of Pennsylvania Press
Philadelphia, Pennsylvania 19104-4112
www.upenn.edu/pennpress

Printed in the United States of America on acid-free paper

10 9 8 7 6 5 4 3 2 1

*Library of Congress Cataloging-in-Publication Data*

Names: Schneider, Eric C., 1951–2017, author.
Title: The ecology of homicide : race, place, and space in postwar Philadelphia / Eric C. Schneider.
Description: 1st edition. | Philadelphia : University of Pennsylvania Press, [2020] | Includes bibliographical references and index.
Identifiers: LCCN 2019052215 | ISBN 978-0-8122-5248-4 (hardcover)
Subjects: LCSH: Homicide—Pennsylvania—Philadelphia—History—20th century. | African Americans—Pennsylvania—Philadelphia—Social conditions. | Philadelphia (Pa.)—Social conditions—History—20th century.
Classification: LCC HV6534.P5 S36 2020 | DDC 364.15209748/1109045—dc23
LC record available at https://lccn.loc.gov/2019052215

For many years my late husband, Eric Schneider, spent one day a week in the Philadelphia City Archives examining every tenth murder case. If our adult children happened to be visiting, he would tell them about the most interesting murder he uncovered that day—something I did not enjoy hearing about. Yet I read drafts of every chapter and learned a lot about our adopted city. I saw him labor over this book for many years and had looked forward to seeing him celebrate its publication. That did not happen.

My children and I will remain forever grateful to Howard Gillette for finishing the book Eric started and hoped to complete before he died. He loved being a historian, he loved teaching and his students, and he loved going to work with colleagues who gave him the time to research and write despite his administrative obligations. Eric's commitment to social and racial justice led him to studies of delinquency, drugs, gangs, and murder. Despite being enmeshed in research on these subjects, he never lost his belief that our nation could do and be better.

—Janet Golden

# Contents

# The Ecology of Homicide

*Foreword*

*Howard Gillette Jr.*

Eric Schneider, an eminent chronicler of what he only semifacetiously referred to as "the dark side of urban life," died March 22, 2017, of a virulent form of cancer. Knowing his illness was terminal, Schneider remained determined nonetheless to finish the book he was working on examining the phenomenon of murder in Philadelphia. For some months he believed he had enough time to complete his draft, but well before he intended to retire from his position at the University of Pennsylvania in December, he took a sudden turn for the worse. At the time of his death, one chapter remained incomplete and further revisions were anticipated in response to comments he had received from a handful of colleagues. At the request of Eric's wife, Janet Golden, I agreed to pick up where Eric left off, not attempting to complete the book as originally anticipated so much as to ensure that the six chapters he had produced were ready for publication and that their collective intent might be further contextualized.

At the heart of the surviving manuscript, Schneider effectively tracked the history of murder in the Quaker City during a critical period from World War II until the early 1980s. Representing both a response to prevailing theory and to contemporary events, in Philadelphia and in other postindustrial centers where tensions between black inner-city residents and police had flared in recent years, the manuscript assumed special power through Schneider's ability to tap the voices of those charged with murder by mining the transcripts of their trials. Looking primarily at the periods leading up to and immediately following the 1966 *Miranda* Supreme Court decision and the shift at about the same time to easy access to guns and the spike of violence that followed, Schneider clearly wanted to provide the historical context that is so often missing in contemporary views of urban violence. Although his chapters do not follow a strict chronology, they nonetheless offer a progression that allows readers to recognize the ways in which the classic urban ghetto became ever more dangerous for those who lived there as the combined effects of concentrated poverty and disinvestment accumulated to sustain and deepen what Schneider calls an ecology of violence.

Not incidentally, as he worked at the University of Pennsylvania, Schneider followed the path of the previous generation's most eminent criminologist, Marvin Wolfgang, whose 1958 study of 550 victims of homicide in Philadelphia formed the foundation for much subsequent research on the prime question he posed about the phenomenon of intraracial homicide: "Why should a quantitatively unknown but presumed greater amount of frustration in the environment of the Negro . . . find aggressive outlet specifically in a high incidence of homicide?" Wolfgang's theory about black-on-black homicide was that it emanated from a subculture of violence, one he shared with the most eminent successor to his study of crime in Philadelphia, Roger Lane.[1] Schneider rejects that proposition in favor of the judgment he made in his earlier book on heroin: "A geography of inequality produced both heroin use and crime. Certain urban neighborhoods concentrated the effects of poverty and racial discrimination and hosted large numbers of the demographic group most prone to both heroin use and street crime: marginalized and isolated young men. These neighborhoods were the by-products of economic development, left over as productive activity moved elsewhere."[2] In this, his work aligned with that of modern sociologists, notably William Julius Wilson and Robert J. Sampson, who argue that such patterns draw most centrally from disparities in community structure as they have been compounded by economic and social inequality. If there are distinct cultural differences between black and white poor, they are largely performative in response to distinct social and institutional conditions, most prominently from police practices intended to maintain order.[3]

When I last met with Eric, about three weeks before his death, our conversation veered between his historical account and the contemporary crisis prompted by police shootings of so many black men. To my comment that we needed more civilian review—a feature notably absent in nearby

Camden, New Jersey, where the police force had been recently reorganized to mixed reviews—Eric had a ready answer: "It didn't work in Philadelphia." Clearly, he had come to believe through years of research on crime that institutional responses, no matter how well meaning, had their limits. The Philadelphia police review board he examines here clearly owed its existence to the ascent of the liberal reformer Richardson Dilworth in the 1950s, and like other historians before him, Schneider describes the limits of mid-twentieth-century liberalism. More hopeful, he thought, were the effects of locally based organizations of the kind he describes in Chapter 5, a phenomenon that sociologist Patrick Sharkey has since brought to national attention.[4] Whatever the solution, Eric's focus remained on experience itself. Eschewing the statistical emphasis of much of the work in the ecological—that is, place-based—study of crime, he manages to bring to life the collective experiences of those charged with murder. The result is a humanizing treatment of murder that may not overturn contemporary theory but will challenge both specialists and the public to recognize and deal with the distinct conditions on the ground that lie at the heart of these tragedies.

Eric knew Philadelphia personally. For some years he lived near the site where graduate student In-Ho Oh was murdered at the edge of the Penn campus in 1958. As a teacher and administrator, Eric followed with interest efforts his university made to secure its own borders while simultaneously trying to act as a good neighbor, a goal it began to achieve only after precipitating the destruction of a nearby vibrant black community through urban renewal, the subject of Chapter 3. Ironically, Oh's cousin, Philadelphia city councilman David Oh, sustained a similar attack outside his Southwest Philadelphia home several months after Eric's death. Fortunate to have survived multiple stab wounds, Councilman Oh acknowledged in subsequent news reports that he had long displayed a portrait of his late cousin in his home, remarking, "As long as I can remember, there was In-Ho Oh." Shortly afterward, another attack—this one fatal—made the news when a white community leader was murdered in the gentrifying Francisville section of the city where, Eric writes, the Moroccos had once defended their territory in the gang wars that escalated in the 1960s. In these, as in so many other ways, the legacy of spatialized violence continued to haunt the city.[5] As progress advanced along with poverty, and as the city's police force maintained a troubled relationship with Philadelphia's more destitute neighborhoods, tensions, even violence, continued to flare.

Eric witnessed the many changes toward the end of his life that signaled Philadelphia's recovery from a long period of decline brought about by the loss of human and monetary capital in the years after World War II when his story begins. He had to be aware especially of the stunning physical changes in the immediate vicinity of Penn as well as other parts of the city, as new investment brought an expanding skyline, an influx of talented young workers, and signs of gentrification, even in unlikely places. He might have acknowledged Philadelphia's case for recruiting Amazon's second national headquarters, and yet he was just as acutely aware of the disparities that left Philadelphia, even on the upswing, with the highest poverty rate among the nation's largest cities. Even as crime inched up nationally, Eric's supposition of the importance of place was confirmed in a September 2017 column in the *New York Times* by criminologist Thomas Abt contending that "to control violence, one must account for it directly by focusing on the small numbers of places, people and behaviors that disproportionately drive the problem."[6] Because that poverty remained concentrated in minority neighborhoods and because the police, despite reforms over the years, still experienced uneasy relations with residents there, Philadelphia's crime problem in the twenty-first century remained problematic at best. Most particularly, the evidence Schneider uncovered affirms the judgment journalist Jill Leovy arrives at in her powerful indictment of the contemporary criminal justice system as "at once oppressive and inadequate." Or, as she puts it, quoting the late scholar William J. Stuntz, "Poor black neighborhoods see too little of the kinds of policing and criminal punishment that do the most good, and too much of the kinds that do the most harm."[7] Eric offers no singular solution here, but as he did in so much of his other work, he forces us to confront the materiality of violence and its distinct manifestation in neighborhoods shaped by a long history of deprivation. Although his writing approach and outlook differed significantly from that of Wolfgang's, it could well be said of Schneider what a colleague attributed to Wolfgang: "Perhaps because Marvin had studied society so thoroughly, including its worst element, he was able to understand human behavior. Instead of producing anger and

despair, this understanding of his fellow human beings engendered tolerance, compassion and hope."[8]


\*    \*    \*


In retrospect, applying the term *postindustrial* to modern Philadelphia
hardly scratches the surface in describing the changes that transformed the
city in the years after World War II. Against the background of the shared
exuberance of victory and the robust economic growth that followed, the
character of the city altered dramatically. Bound to no one portion of the
industrial sector, the city's diversified economy blunted for a while the cen-
trifugal forces that were pulling big plants out of the cities they had once
dominated. That changed in the 1960s, when Philadelphia lost some 90,000
jobs, fully 8 percent of its employment base. Seventy percent of jobs lost
were in manufacturing. Coupled with the outward pull of the suburbs,
where the attractions of a rich consumer economy beckoned, losses in
employment were matched by an equally dramatic dip in population: the
loss of some 50,000 residents. That pattern only accelerated in the following
decade. Not incidentally, the homicide rate escalated. Having hovered at
5.7 per 100,000 persons into the early 1960s, it increased by 300 percent
between 1965 and 1974.[9]

Such changes were masked for a time by the excitement over yet
another alteration in known experience: the overturning of a Republican
political machine that had dominated the city even through the New Deal
and war years when other industrial centers had long since fallen under
Democratic control. Seeking to modernize the city and keep it economically
competitive, a coalition of lawyers, bankers, business representatives, and
civic organizations strove to improve efficiency in government, root out
corruption, and improve professionalism in city departments, a campaign
that cumulated in adoption of a new city charter in 1951. The election of
one of their members as mayor, Joseph Clark, the same year ushered in not
just Democratic control of the city that has lasted ever since, but also a
wave of additional reform measures in a city still bearing the reputation so

properly solidified by journalist Lincoln Steffens at the outset of the century as "corrupt and contented."[10] In addition to introducing civilian review of the police, the new regime embraced an ambitious program of physical rehabilitation aimed not just at renewing venerable city neighborhoods but also at reversing the forces that were encouraging the abandonment of city homes and businesses.

The years after the war should have offered the city's black residents, their population swollen from 385,000 in 1950 to 600,000 in 1980, a boost. Long restricted to only a few residential enclaves, primarily in the area south of the central city the distinguished scholar W. E. B. DuBois had brought to light in his landmark 1899 study *The Philadelphia Negro*, African Americans now had additional residential choices as whites abandoned the city in ever greater numbers. Supported in their expectations that triumphing over the enemy would be a double victory, for securing rights at home as well as defeating the enemy abroad, they could count the advent of a human relations commission and the subsequent formation of a fair housing commission, among other nascent civil rights measures, as proof of their confidence.

Such victories proved limited, however. Despite the good intentions behind city measures aimed at fair treatment, in practice they lacked either sufficient will or enforcement power to make a difference. Although industrial employment had opened to some degree during the war under federal pressures to practice nondiscrimination, they had been blunted by Republican control of the city during the war and by company decisions to dismiss black workers once peace had been secured. While it was true that new housing opportunities were opening up, they were anything but random. While white workers of modest means held fast to their own neighborhoods, despite the first blows from disinvestment in once-thriving industrial areas such as Kensington, African Americans were likely to find solutions to the overcrowding they had experienced in the war years largely in transitional areas. A prime destination was the area on the north side of the central city where a once-thriving vice district known as the Tenderloin had been cleaned up by an earlier generation of reformers. Although North Philadelphia's black population had grown to nearly 100,000 before the war, it attracted close to another 70,000 during the 1940s and exceeded 200,000 by 1960.

This, then, was a new kind of ghetto analyzed most graphically by sociologist William Julius Wilson in his 1987 book *The Truly Disadvantaged.*[11] Unlike the community DuBois described encompassing the full range of professional and working-class African Americans, North Philadelphia became home primarily to the poorest among the city's black residents. As both their numbers and their marginality to the mainstream economy deepened, the area's reputation—and by proxy that of its residents— deteriorated. By the early 1960s, North Philadelphia had the city's highest poverty and unemployment rates and fraught relations with the police. On August 28, 1964, those relations reached a low point as a scuffle with police at a busy intersection at the heart of a portion of North Philadelphia frequently referred to by public authorities and the press as "the Jungle" escalated into three days of civil disorder. By the time peace had been restored, hundreds had been arrested and injured, two killed, and widespread damage inflicted on commercial properties.[12]

Leaving no doubt about the association between crime and an area marked by physical deprivation, a contemporary assessment of the rioting commissioned by the American Jewish Committee asserted, "Crimes of a violent and emotional nature are associated with its residents, and nearly one-half of all major offenses in the city in 1963 were committed within its precincts." Pointing to an unemployment rate double that of the city's, at 13 percent, high dropout rates, and as many as thirty-three gangs rumbling on North Philadelphia's turf, author Lenora Berson cited police reports that 90 percent of those indicted for looting or violation of the mayor's curfew during the riot had a previous arrest record. Such conditions, she argued, served as fodder for confrontation. "Unlike white, middle-class children," she wrote, "Negro youngsters do not grow up thinking of the policeman on the corner as their friend. Most Negroes look upon the policeman as the brutal enforcer of the white man's laws—laws that have been used for three centuries to keep the black man down."[13]

As happened in so many other cities, civil disturbances brought new attention, and President Lyndon Johnson's Model Cities program was directed largely at North Philadelphia in the years immediately following the Columbia Avenue confrontation. But the program never took off and was quickly abandoned. Rather, an aggressive urban renewal program effected during the same period resulted in the loss of 40,000 housing units,

further setting North Philadelphia apart from the center city, where rehabilitation had been preferred to demolition. By the mid-1980s, North Philadelphia had twice the concentration of nonwhites it had in 1950.[14]

For more than a generation, from the time when the Great Migration
brought growing numbers of African Americans to the city, public authorities had largely tolerated minor violations of the law as long as they did not
affect the white community. Bearing the burden of being closed out of so
many sectors of the economy, either by overt prejudice or by customs that
maintained white control over whole occupation sectors through the hiring
of friends and relatives, African Americans in great numbers gravitated to
an underground economy. Labeled "business under a cloud" in St. Clair
Drake and Horace Cayton's landmark study of Chicago's black belt, organized vice, whether gambling, prostitution, or some form of bartering, survived with public sanction to the extent that police officers looked the other
way as long as they were paid off. No African American was too proper to
escape such treatment, it appears. Michael Nutter, who served as Philadelphia mayor from 2008 until 2016, recalled that as a Catholic school–
educated teenager, he was pulled out of a car while parked with a date in
Fairmount Park and told his problem had gone away once he had passed
along a five-dollar bill.[15] That such systemic corruption survived the
"reform years" associated with Clark and his chosen successor as mayor,
Richardson Dilworth, was revealed in a detailed and devastating state report
issued in 1974. Rejecting the defense that police violations constituted the
marginal actions of "a few bad apples," the introduction to the nearly nine-
hundred-page report identified the single biggest roadblock to institutional
reforms as "the repeated failure of the Department leadership and the City
Administration to admit that corruption exists on a widespread, systematic
basis."[16]

Police payouts may have exempted some African Americans from prosecution, but they did not ensure the kind of protection of property or
person that was routinely afforded white neighborhoods. Indeed, earlier in
the century, efforts African Americans made to draw attention to the need
for uniform measures of public safety in their communities had the unin-
tended effect of furthering the association of crime with a black presence.
Even as black critics in Philadelphia directed attention to the racist practices
that fostered social instability, including crime, crime statistics continued

to be cited as evidence of bad behavior in need of suppression.[17] The contemporary realization that African Americans endure a double bind of unwanted police attention to a black presence—through such invasive tactics as search and frisk and racial profiling—without the kind of uniform commitment to public safety extended to white neighborhoods has informed Philadelphia for generations.[18] It informs Schneider's study and confirms the importance African Americans living in such geographically confined areas as North Philadelphia attached to the practice of arming themselves.

In the transitional period Schneider writes about, the pervasiveness of gun violence had yet to materialize, hence the widespread presence of knives as weapons. Urban renewal was still seen as part of a reform agenda, making over areas in decline so other uses could flourish. The impact on the expansion of the University of Pennsylvania, as one example, had not yet been recognized as destroying established patterns of black settlement and the devastating effects that followed from displacement in other parts of the city. Schneider had every intent of writing one additional chapter, on the ways African Americans moved into organized crime, a phenomenon closely tied to the business of drugs, which he wrote about in his other work. That study will have to come from someone else. What he leaves us is a powerful link, between that moment of promise following World War II and the very mixed assessment of the contemporary city. Philadelphia today is the poorest among the nation's large cities. A prominent and successful black middle class notwithstanding, much of that poverty can be identified with areas of black residence, neighborhoods where issues of crime and the administration of justice remain uneven and contested. The murder rate—still unacceptably high and still predominantly associated with areas Schneider identifies as characterized by an ecology of violence—challenges every positive association we attribute to a place we like to call the City of Brotherly Love.[19]

*Preface*

I began this book in 2006 when I realized that I lived in the city with the highest homicide rate among America's ten largest cities. Philadelphia, or "Killadelphia" as it is sometimes referred to in the media, has a persistently high rate of homicide that has defied the decline in murder that occurred elsewhere in the country. Philadelphia's homicides did not occur on a random basis throughout the city; rather, like murders elsewhere, they were both racialized and spatialized, concentrating among a low-income African American population living within particular neighborhoods. In Philadelphia, African Americans account for 78 percent of the approximately 9,200 individuals murdered since 1988; African American males account for 68 percent, and African American males between the ages of eighteen and forty account for 52 percent of the city's homicide victims over that period. Since more than 90 percent of all murders are committed intraracially, the conclusion is inescapable that murder is a black man's disease. I want to understand why.

Black-on-black homicide over time has become a fraught topic, used variously to justify and to criticize police actions that disproportionately single out the most frequent victims of such violence: young, black urban men. To make such crime the object of analysis might be objected to, on the one hand, for neglecting white victims or, on the other, for possibly reinforcing stereotypes about African American male violence based on data gathered from an inherently racist criminal justice system. These objections are without merit. Social problems are not solved through silence, and the data about murder are incontrovertible. One virtue to studying murder lies in its materiality: murder, unlike many other crimes, can be counted reliably. Each killing produces an artifact, a body, that the state has a vested interest in accounting for. That body is weighed, measured, photographed, dissected, and the cause, time, and means of death determined, producing a record that is largely impervious to legal and definitional change. Biases abound in the criminal justice process and therefore in criminal justice statistics, but biases do not produce bodies. Murderers do.

Murder has generally had the highest "clearance rates" among crimes. Police departments take pride in their ability to solve murder cases, with big city departments expecting to clear about 80 percent or more of their cases, although that percentage has been dropping over time. Police clear a case when they have a reasonable suspicion as to the perpetrator and can charge a suspect, even if an indictment cannot be procured for various reasons. For criminologists and fellow-traveling historians, this kind of high probability crime is the gold standard for analyzing murder.

For my analysis I use a different standard. I rely on a sample of homicide trial transcripts—cases that not only were "solved" by police but also were sufficiently strong to gain an indictment in a magistrate's hearing and then go to trial. As the work of the Innocence Project has shown, the criminal justice process is far from infallible, even in our own time, but at least the virtue of a trial is that a judge and jury publicly evaluate the evidence, which a defendant has the right to contest. Because about half the period I study came before the Supreme Court issued its famous *Miranda* decision in 1966—a period in which police routinely failed to advise suspects that they had a right to an attorney, moved them from lockup to lockup in high-profile cases in order to hide them from their families, and just as routinely used coercion (the "third degree") to extort confessions—many of the defendants I followed faced particularly steep obstacles in receiving just sentences. Acknowledging that convictions were the result of a flawed system may raise questions about the guilt of a particular suspect in a particular case or about the legality of a process. Nonetheless, such prejudice does not change the fact of a murder or the artifact that a trial must account for. Comparing the defense and the prosecution accounts of a murder provides me an opportunity to assess responsibility, much as a juror in a case is expected to do. And from that process emerges a larger picture of the world out of which the victim emerged.

Prosecutors and defenders craft narrow cases, often leaving out larger explanations that might provide an opening for an opponent by suggesting incriminating or exculpatory factors. And judges urge attorneys to keep to the immediate "facts" of the case. Justice is then apportioned individually, and responsibility is measured in a number of years—or lifetimes—that a guilty defendant serves. But the cumulative effect of so many trials over so many years is broadly social, revealing an ecology of violence, bound in place over time. As sociologists Brendan O'Flaherty and Rajiv Sethi have demonstrated so forcefully, not only has the racially distinct pattern of murder persisted for generations, but it has been highly correlated with segregation.[1] The resulting ecology—the spacing and interdependence of people and institutions—for those trying to understand modern patterns of violence is a phenomenon that must be reckoned with.

Ultimately this is not a book about legal process, key trials, or even murder itself, although I will have something to say about all three. As a historian, I want to understand the ecology of homicide, its social and spatial concentration, for the way it facilitates the reading of urban history. My sample of trial transcripts produces an intimate record, a set of narratives, with which to understand the lives of poor people, the history of a great city, and the soul of violence itself.

## Chapter 1

# Dancing with Knives

## The Ecological Structure of African American Homicide in Postwar Philadelphia

## The Problem of Homicide

Why do African American men kill one another, as well as others, with such alarming frequency? Both historical and contemporary studies show that African American men are by far the largest number of victims and of perpetrators of urban homicide,[1] and those studies that have disaggregated the data indicate that urban homicide has clustered in a handful of black neighborhoods.[2] In other words, homicide has been both socially and spatially concentrated in African American communities. In Philadelphia from 1948 to 1952, the homicide rate for whites was 1.9 per 100,000 persons, while for African Americans the rate was 22.5, producing an overall homicide rate of 5.7 per 100,000 for the city. Homicide among black men has driven the city's homicide rate since World War II, if not before.[3] The data are incontrovertible; the question is how do we account for them?[4] Some scholars have postulated that a subculture of violence, created in the South among whites and African Americans, moved north with the Great Migration.[5] Since the late nineteenth century, the South has had the highest regional homicide rates in the United States, and few would deny the existence of a peculiarly southern worldview.[6] A southern culture of violence would have been most apparent in northern cities during the 1940s and 1950s, when the wartime and postwar migration deposited tens of thousands of southern African Americans in northern ghettoes. Yet overall, homicide rates among African Americans, while much higher than those among whites, were declining in this period and only began their meteoric rise in the mid-1960s among African Americans too young to have been exposed directly to a southern culture of violence. This raises the question, at what point would a southern culture of violence become "northern"? The view of culture inherent in this question is largely static, seeing it as simply handed down from one generation to the next, like the family Bible. Moreover, efforts to identify southern values that might support homicidal violence have failed.[7] As an attempt to explain African American homicide in the several decades after World War II, this variant of subcultural theory is unsatisfactory, both empirically and theoretically.

A second stance posits that a subculture of violence characterizes inner-city communities and is rooted in a distinctive value system and a personality structure that are at odds with those found in mainstream society.[8] But subcultural theorists have difficulty explaining how a particular set of values arose, how and why they changed, and how they can be reconciled with sudden shifts, such as the doubling of the national homicide rate in the 1960s, that affected both blacks and whites. In addition, most scholars now see culture as fluid and performative, something that articulates with the social setting in which it is performed and thus something that changes over time.[9] The subculture of violence theory fails this test.

Other scholars see value systems, such as a "code of the street," developing in response to a local social setting and therefore not indicative of an independent value structure. The street code may involve only a minority of residents, but it is so threatening and so dominates the public sphere that virtually all community members must learn how to negotiate it. Such practice, with its ties in particular to the assertion of manhood, sociologist Elijah Anderson argues, is closely tied to the social ecology that has brought extreme poverty to ghetto areas as a result of structural change.[10] In another version, violence is seen as instrumental and situational, something that is employed rationally by a few actors and offers them protective value.[11] Both of these views are suggestive, but because they are rooted in an analysis of the crack cocaine trade, they are theorized too narrowly to be applied to the whole postwar era.

Homicide is a gendered activity, but efforts to explain homicide in terms of gender are also unsatisfying. Men commit approximately 85–90 percent of homicides, regardless of time, place, or culture. The evolutionary psychologists Martin Daly and Margo Wilson, examining familial homicides, argue for its basis in natural selection: spouses, in-laws, and nonnatal children (i.e., stepchildren) rather than blood kin account for most of these murders.[12] However, given wide variation in homicide rates across time, place, and cultures, what is constant (male gender) is much less interesting than what is variable, namely, the rates at which homicides are committed. Historian David Courtwright sees gender ratios rather than gender per se as what counts: societies where family formation is impossible because of an excess of one gender or the other are characterized by high rates of violence. Low marriage rates reinforce homosocial bonds and the male irresponsibility associated with violence, a trend most apparent on the frontier West and in the modern inner city.[13] As historian Jeffrey Adler notes, however, this argument fails to explain the experience of European immigrant groups (Poles, for example) at the turn of the twentieth century with high gender imbalances but low homicide rates.[14]

Other scholars have explained the history of homicide by referring to Norbert Elias's concept of a "civilizing process." According to Elias and his many followers, the high homicide rates that characterized premodern European societies have declined over the past five centuries as states have secured borders and monopolized force, political participation has legitimated state authority, markets have embedded individuals in relationships of mutual dependence, and, most important, habits of thinking, acting, and behaving have become more self-restrained.[15] These historians resort to "American exceptionalism" to explain the much higher rates of American homicide, which would make African Americans more exceptional still.[16] However, as historian Randolph Roth has pointed out, the decline in homicide in Western Europe was marked by great variation over time, and advances in medical treatment explain much of what appears to be a decline in homicide. That is, hospital emergency rooms now save many lives that in earlier years would have been lost, which reduces the overall difference in homicide rates between premodern and modern societies. Efforts to apply Elias's theory in the United States have also proved problematic if only because of regional variations in homicide, rural-urban differences, and even differences among cities at the same point in time, all suggesting that the civilizing process, if at work at all, operates at such a level of abstraction that it is useless for understanding the very phenomenon it purports to explain.[17] Modernization theory, which links the decline in violence to the rise of Protestantism and individualism, is another variant of this argument.[18] One might note, however, that Protestantism and individualism have never been at odds with violence in the United States.

Sociologist Loic Wacquant, in accounting for the increase in violence in urban black communities, argues that the civilizing process has actually gone into reverse. He associates violence with a "decivilizing process" in which institutional life has declined, the economy has become informalized (employment in the formal sector of the economy has been replaced by short-term, episodic employment and the rise of an underground economy), and the state, with the exception of the police and the criminal justice system, has largely disappeared.[19] While I agree with Wacquant's conclusions about the modern inner city, his version of history is wrong. Wacquant posits a romanticized golden age "communal ghetto" in the mid-twentieth century, itself presumably the product of a civilizing process, which is contradicted by the high, very noncommunal homicide rates of the postwar period.

Historian Roger Lane's "industrial exclusion" thesis compares the historical experiences of African Americans and various European immigrant groups and proposes that the latter's inclusion in the industrial economy lowered homicide. According to Lane, the demands of tending soberly to industrial machinery for sixty-hour work weeks, combined with limited access to alcohol, reinforced habits of self-discipline and prevented congregation on street corners and outside bars except for the weekends, while the expansion of urban school systems forced male children to ingrain this same discipline. African Americans, Lane argues, never acquired "industrial virtues." Systematically excluded from the industrial economy except during times of extreme labor shortages or during strikes, African American homicide rates declined during the 1940s and 1950s when the industrial economy briefly opened up before jobs were permanently exported to the suburbs, the Sunbelt, and eventually overseas.[20] And yet homicide rates also declined during the nineteenth century in areas with little or no industry and only modest school attendance.[21] Lane cannot explain why homicide rates have diverged so dramatically in the recent past: unlike Detroit, Philadelphia, and St. Louis, New York and Los Angeles have enjoyed remarkable declines in violent crime, and these cities are not reindustrializing. Something else has been at work.

Criminologist Gary LaFree links the rise in violent crime in the late twentieth century to a crisis in the legitimacy of American institutions. The dramatic increase in economic inequality during the 1960s and 1970s, the decline in the traditional family, and growing mistrust of government are all correlated with rising rates of robbery and murder, while increased spending on welfare programs, education, and incarceration are correlated with stabilization or modest declines in violent crime as alternate institutions were developed.[22] This hypothesis seems clearly applicable to African Americans who have suffered from economic inequality, have had little reason to trust governmental institutions, and have had family structures under increasing stress in the postwar period. When extended backward in time, however, the correlations that appear in the postwar period are no longer clear, with the possible exception of the political legitimacy argument. Randolph Roth argues that low homicide rates are associated with a belief that government is stable and just, with trust in the probity of public officials, with the existence of "fellow feeling" within groups, and with the perception that one is part of a legitimate social hierarchy. The crux of the argument is that homicide rates have varied historically with faith in government: sometimes this faith is in local government and at others in national government, depending on the situation Roth wishes to explain.[23] In the late 1990s, for instance, homicide rates diverged dramatically in Philadelphia and in New York City—staying high in the locale with the African American mayor and dropping in the city with a conservative white Republican one, both under the same presidential administration. Place clearly matters, but the argument for a link between attitudes toward government and homicide in the twentieth-century city seems tenuous at best. To understand the root and cause of homicide, we need to look at the phenomenon itself.

## Jim Crow City

Within specific locations, such as Philadelphia, black and white homicide rates moved up and down more or less in tandem, showing that the same larger historical forces affect both. Despite variation over time, the rate among African Americans was consistently much higher than that among whites, and this persistent difference requires explanation. A number of scholars have linked high crime rates either to segregation or to the more recent concentration of poverty and social isolation of the poor.[24] Here I propose to look at the 1940s, to show how homicide was linked to the process of ghettoization in the era before the poor became socially and spatially isolated, during the period Wacquant has identified as the "communal ghetto."

The process of ghettoization—funneling a stigmatized group into spatial enclaves preserved formally by government policy and informally by the actions of the majority community along its borderlands—muted the impact of events that drove down homicide elsewhere in American society during the postwar period. The exclusion of African Americans from industrial employment may have been declining during the war under pressure from civil rights groups, but with peace those opportunities dried up. As government housing policies lured working- and middle-class whites to areas of new settlement and redevelopment policies further concentrated African Americans in areas of lowered opportunities for legitimate employment, vice markets flourished, pulling both residents and police into their orbit.[25] Lacking access to regular employment and thus deprived of traditional roles as breadwinners, black men exercised their masculinity more readily and more visibly through participation in street life, confrontations among peers, and dominance over women, all of which led easily to violence.[26] Undoubtedly aware of prevailing bias, black men had no basis for a belief in the criminal justice system either to protect them from the vicissitudes of a volatile world or to settle their grievances.[27] Logic alone prompted them to rely only on themselves and to carry knives or guns for self-protection. They did so in distinct areas, for the color line in the postwar city remained clearly drawn, maintained not just by custom but by the violence African Americans encountered as they ventured into white residential areas.[28] While pacification of city streets occurred most obviously in elite and middle-class sections of the metropolis, working-class and poor neighborhoods relied more on informal social controls that were stressed by racial transition. Here, where both normative and institutional restraints on violence were tentative at best, homicide among low-income African Americans became a social production of the segregating city.

This emphasis on the ecological structuring of behavior derives from the Chicago School of Sociology emphasis on social ecology, which contemporary sociologists William Julius Wilson and Robert Sampson have revived by relating ecological dissimilarities with incidences of spatial inequality by race.[29] But individuals are not just acted upon by their social settings; they create them. Historians, with their emphasis on agency, look to the role of human actors in making, resisting, and responding to social environments. While this perspective is usually applied to social activists, murderers are no different than any other agents except in the objects of their agency. Murder is clearly the result of a social ecology, a social situation (a "habitus" to use Pierre Bourdieu's terminology), but it is simultaneously determined by the actor.[30] The assertion of masculinity appears frequently as a proximate cause of violence because it was through the creation and presentation of self that these actors internalized and reproduced the ecological structure of violence. To put the matter simply, murderers are both the product and the producers of a social ecology of violence, as I hope to demonstrate through specific case histories below.

An analysis of the transcripts of 195 trials for homicide (first-and second-degree murder and voluntary manslaughter) that took place in Philadelphia between 1940 and 1949 provides evidence for my claims.[31] The race of the defendants and the victims can be identified in nearly 90 percent of the cases, and 83 percent of the defendants and 78 percent of the victims were African American.[32] With transcripts that often run to the hundreds of pages, these trials provide a unique window into the relationship between homicide and ghettoization in Philadelphia during the 1940s.

At first it seems difficult to relate the mundane nature of these homicides to any larger theme either in American history or in the literature on homicide. Nearly 40 percent of the homicide cases resulted from disputes among friends or acquaintances (38.9 percent) and a third of the murders (32.8 percent) involved a family, spousal, or relationship killing, as homicide was turned inward toward intimate others. Disputes among strangers, often over apparently trivial matters, accounted for only about a fifth of the homicides. Only a few (6.6 percent) involved a felony, such as a robbery or holdup, where premeditation was established and where violence might be more clearly interpreted as instrumental.[33] Certainly no one reading these materials would be convinced of rational-choice theories in which criminals weigh the odds of punishment and calculate the potential gains of crime before pulling the trigger.[34]

The most common form of homicide occurred between friends, usually after a bout of drinking. These killings happened in the hundreds of bars that dotted the city's streets ("taprooms" had their own classification in Wolfgang's study, and 8 percent of the city's murders occurred there), especially in poor and working-class neighborhoods, or on the streets outside as victim and murderer stumbled their way home, or in someone's living room. Easy conviviality gave way suddenly to outbursts of rage, and men carrying weapons faced off over accumulated grievances normally hidden under a guise of friendship but now violently exposed. For example, John Byrd murdered his friend Shorty Lewis as they walked down the street arguing after Shorty refused him money for a bottle of wine. Byrd told Shorty to stop joking, and "one word led to another about me being high." Byrd explained that he stabbed Shorty because he had treated him so many times and Shorty never treated him back, a clear violation of a male code of mutuality and generosity. That the murder was not intentional did not stop Byrd from bragging about it. When he saw a female acquaintance, Adelle Hall, he threatened her, showing her a bloodstain on the pavement and telling her, "I killed that nigger Shorty, and I will give you the same thing." Although Byrd worked for a butcher, perhaps accounting for his familiarity with knives, he also had a criminal past that suggested familiarity with a criminal underworld as well: he had a long series of arrests for gambling, drugs, disorderly conduct, breaking and entering, and larceny, and he said he had carried a knife because he had gone to a dance and "men dance with knives."[35]

Of course, if one expected others to be armed in a location where no external authority kept order, where alcohol fueled both conviviality and its opposite, and where fights might break out among competitive males seeking to assert their dominance over others or gain the attention of females, going unarmed could be considered foolish. A reputation for violence was useful to counter potential threats posed by others and, less instrumentally, was part of one's masculine identity, one that had to be constantly asserted and defended. Alcohol and edginess triggered the sort of incidents that cost Shorty Lewis his life and sent John Byrd to prison for an eight-to-sixteen-year stretch for second-degree murder. But it was the social setting—the insecurity of the neighborhood and the precariously established masculinity negotiated by the men who lived there—that established a social ecology of violence.[36]

While Byrd and Lewis were participants in a criminal underworld where a resort to violence might be anticipated, even those who had no criminal pasts routinely carried weapons and reacted when their manliness was threatened. Ernest Jordan stabbed Allen Latney, whom he had visited nearly every day since childhood. The pair got into an argument when Latney refused to move over in the back seat of a car to let Jordan and a young woman in. "I came out and walked over to the car and said to Allen, 'Allen, straighten up, I got a girl coming out too,' and told him to sit up straight so that I and my girl can get into the car too. So he cursed me and told me to get out and take a walk and he reached for his back pocket and I went into my pocket and flipped my knife open and cut him in the throat." Latney started bleeding profusely, and the young people bundled him back into the car and drove him to the hospital, even notifying police of the incident once they warned Jordan to get out of the car and flee. But Latney died two hours after being dropped off in the emergency room, and Jordan faced a second-degree homicide charge.[37] By disrespecting his friend, cursing at Jordan in front of a woman he hoped to impress (and who was not his wife), Allen Latney made a fatal mistake that not even the claims of lifelong friendship could overcome. Such homicides were not limited to African American neighborhoods—poor white men also killed their friends in alcohol-induced bouts of violence (43 percent of white homicides between 1948 and 1952)—but acquaintance homicides happened even more frequently among African Americans (52 percent of the homicides involving black males), evidence of the precariousness of masculine identity in the ghettoizing city.[38]

Male honor was at the root of many killings, as men acted as patriarchal protectors of women they perceived as vulnerable—and who might not have other sources of protection than vigilant menfolk. Frank Newton stabbed Harry Brown after Brown repeatedly accused the thirty-one-year-old of paying inappropriate attention to the teenaged daughter of a neighbor ("I know you're Mary's nigger") and called him a "rotten son-of-a-bitch." The last exchange led to a fistfight in the street that ended with

Newton pulling a knife.[39] Archie Burney, Richard Crump, and Irwin Hobbs got into a fight with another man after stopping him from going out with the intoxicated wife of a mutual friend. When Hobbs stopped Jean on the street around 2:00 a.m. and told her to go home, her companion, James Shivers, told Hobbs to mind his own business. The dispute sputtered out, and Burney, Crump, and Hobbs continued on to a diner and placed their orders. About ten minutes later, Shivers appeared outside the window and beckoned Hobbs to come out. When Hobbs ignored him, Shivers entered, saying, "If any one of you fellows wants to fight, come on and fight." After another exchange of words, Shivers suddenly reached inside his coat, pulling out an iron rod, and beat Hobbs over the head and knocked Burney into the lunch counter and onto the floor. Someone swung a chair, causing Shivers to stagger, while Burney grabbed a knife and plunged it into Shivers's stomach. By then the police arrived and called for an ambulance, with Shivers explaining that the men had tried to take a girl away from him. Several witnesses in the diner all testified that Shivers had started the fight, so the jury accepted Burney's assertion of self-defense.[40]

Shivers's actions made the jury's decision easy, but at a time (1942) when many husbands and fathers were leaving for war and women enjoyed an unchaperoned nightlife, jurors probably sympathized with men who seemed to be acting chivalrously. Hobbs explained to the jury that he hoped that if his wife were in a vulnerable situation, a friend might intervene on her behalf. (It is notable that these accounts were told solely from the perspective of the male defendants, and neither Mary nor Jean testified during the trials.) On dangerous neighborhood streets, especially late at night, men looked out for each other and prepared to act violently to protect the interests of their friends.

Disputes with strangers were very similar to those among friends, occurring frequently in the same type of locations, involving alcohol, and originating largely for the same reasons. Chance encounters might not damage one's standing among peers, but they went to the heart of one's self-identity, as a man not to be trifled with. Even as minor an occurrence as an accidental brush of shoulders on a street could lead to violence, as when "Sonny" Clark charged into a pool room to confront the teenager who had jostled him. Refusing to accept an apology and calling the young men punks ("you jitterbugs, I will kick you all in the ass"), the older Clark went after the boys who showed restraint and kept retreating. The show of submission did no good and perhaps even encouraged Clark to assert his dominance over the youths he viewed so contemptuously. The "houseman" intervened, telling Clark to accept the apology and forget it, but Clark ordered him out of the way and punched Joseph Harvey, who then pulled a pistol and fired as he fell to the ground, killing Clark.[41] Since Harvey was backing away and Clark was intent on harming someone, anyone, in the group, the court found Harvey guilty of voluntary manslaughter, sentencing him only to time served up to twenty-three months. Clark's violence makes little sense except in a neighborhood social ecology where manhood depended on toughness, the ability to intimidate others, and the readiness to use violence to impose one's will on inferiors. The fact that Clark was a well-known "badman," a neighborhood Stagger Lee with a reputation for violence, determined both Clark's aggressiveness and the teenagers' fearful retreat.[42]

The use of a gun in the Clark homicide was somewhat unusual. Only a third of Philadelphia's homicides in this period were committed with guns, according to Wolfgang, and there were no major racial distinctions (34 percent of black homicides versus 30 percent of white) in their use. But about half of the homicides involving African Americans (47 percent) were committed with knives or piercing instruments while whites were much more likely to beat someone to death than to knife someone (42 percent versus 17 percent).[43] This distinctive racial pattern indicates the insecurity in African American neighborhoods, where individuals had to rely on themselves for protection. When African Americans confronted each other in a bar, on the street, or in a home, they were much more likely than whites (81 percent vs. 47 percent) to be armed with either a gun or a knife. While fistfights and stompings clearly could cause death, the use of a weapon increased the odds of a fatal outcome. Carrying weapons may have increased feelings of personal security, but they guaranteed an environment of social insecurity that was an essential contributor to the ecology of violence.

Weapons were a stock in trade for people dealing in illegal goods and services. Disputes over dice games, over payouts after someone hit a number, or in thinly disguised brothels and speakeasies accounted for 10 percent of the homicide cases and indicate the importance of the vice trade in the underground economy of black neighborhoods. There was no appeal to authority here, no mediator to settle a grievance or negotiate a debt repayment: everything was handled mano a mano. "Bow Jack" Jackson shot Willie Smith after an argument about drawing a card in a game of "skin." Both men reached for the same card, and "Little Willie" Smith said, "Before I let you take advantage of me, I will kill one of you all." The other card players told Smith that it was Jackson's card, but Smith refused to listen: "He said, 'I will kill you, motherfucker,'" and jumped up but was restrained by the other men. Jackson left the game, and about five minutes later Smith left as well. Jackson may have been waiting for him, because the other gamblers heard some shots almost immediately and ran outside: "I looked out the door about half a minute. Then I seen Willie Smith stumble around the corner and fall in the street." Jackson argued that Smith had a gun and that when Smith drew his revolver, they fought over it. "When he hit me, I turned him loose. Then he swung off to shoot me, and I fired the pistol." The jury acquitted Jackson, even though he had time to leave the scene without confronting Smith and, based on his own account, probably had a gun in his possession.[44] The jury apparently thought it should leave the small world of West Philadelphia hustlers and gamblers to run according to its own social codes, which of course only further encouraged men to carry weapons and use them.[45]

The second most common form of homicide—domestic or relationship violence—had its own patterns. This was the main form of homicide in which black women featured prominently as murderers. Thirty-two African American men (29.3 percent of black male defendants) and seventeen African American women (58.6 percent of black female defendants) were charged in spousal, family, or relationship murders, including three women charged with infanticide. Whereas domestic homicides with white male defendants clustered in 1945 and 1946 (only five cases) and were clearly related to postwar adjustments between returning veterans and their spouses, domestic homicide among African Americans continued at a steady pace throughout the decade, indicating a more entrenched form of violence. Most of these cases, including the ones with female defendants, involved violent men who were abusing their spouses or girlfriends, leading to the death of one or the other. Many of these cases were characterized by long-standing abuse, exacerbated by alcohol. Relationships were strained and sometimes collapsed under the pressure of poverty and irregular employment. The interventions of friends or relatives were ineffectual, only seeming to delay a fatal outburst.

Oliver and Louise Euell had a history of violence throughout their seventeen-year marriage. Oliver had been stabbed with a butcher knife in the arm, head, and nose one time when Louise was drunk, and on another occasion, he had beaten her seriously enough to be arrested. Their son had been removed from the home and sent to the Catholic Protectory for his safety. A drunken quarrel over two dollars spent on ale led Oliver Euell to beat his wife to death.[46] Mary Wilson told her husband, Arthur, that she was leaving him because she did not want to kill him. The two quarreled over money, and Mary had left her husband several times: "I in turn, as soon as I could learn her location, I asked her to come back with me and she did," Arthur asserted. "She leaves me because she says I don't make enough money and . . . I can't afford to get another job because I am on parole." After she told him she was leaving for good, Arthur pulled out a knife and slit her throat.[47] Men, imbued with patriarchal notions of family, asserted romantic but deadly claims over women who seemed to be slipping away. Such claims should be understood in the context of a social ecology where violence and masculinity were intertwined. Men displayed prowess through dominance over others, and violence was integral to that display.

Social constructions of patriarchy demanded that men support their wives, even if they found it impossible to do so. For example, eighteen-year-old Hazel Johnson had come to Philadelphia from North Carolina to visit her sister, Marilyn, who was employed as a domestic. Hazel, who had been married at fifteen, liked the big city life, and her husband, Hilbert, followed her north to look for work but had difficulty making ends meet. Marilyn was asked in court if the couple fought over Hazel's clothing and other purchases, but she said no "because it was understood that I was buying her clothes." The twenty-three-year-old Hilbert worked as a day laborer and could not afford to splurge on his wife, but it no doubt rankled that his sister-in-law provided the things he could not. The Johnsons' quarreling got bad enough that Hazel asked her sister for carfare to return home to North Carolina because Hilbert was threatening to kill her. Marilyn came over and asked Hilbert what was the matter with him, but he said nothing, seething silently and perhaps fearing further emasculation in the eyes of the two women. Hazel warned Marilyn that Hilbert had a knife on him, but Marilyn thought that he was calm and headed home after inviting the two to come for dinner the next evening. Hilbert told police the argument continued after Marilyn left. "Hazel then struck at me and I slapped her. Hazel then said I am not going to live with you anymore, then we started down the stairs to the first floor and when we got to the third step from the bottom, she stopped and said, 'Hilbert why not just let's break it up?' I then took the knife out of my right-side pocket and opened it . . . and I said I am not going to argue with you, then I cut her, I really did." Asked why, he replied, "I love the girl and did not want her messing with anyone else."[48] Similar phrases appeared again and again in domestic/relationship homicides as men, stuck on a romantic ideal that clashed with the realities of life as unskilled laborers or casual workers in a Philadelphia ghetto, tried to assert permanent possession over their wives and girlfriends.

In other incidents, women killed their abusive husbands or boyfriends or incited others to attempt it for them, but the circumstances were nearly identical to those in which men were the perpetrators. A history of violent abuse led to these homicides, but instead of a man going too far and killing a spouse, these women drew a line that an abusive partner finally crossed. After Andrew Vance beat Mary Jones with a rubber hose, she asked her twenty-four-year-old son, Melvin, for help. Melvin showed up with several friends and asked Vance why he was beating his mother. It is not clear if threats were exchanged, but the next day when Melvin returned to help his mother move out, Vance greeted him and his friends with a blast from his twelve-gauge shotgun, killing one of the young men.[49]

Police officer Edward McBride found Sam Minor dead in bed after being summoned by neighbors. He thought Minor might have been unconscious, but when he went to shake him, "I noticed a pool of blood by his right shoulder. Lifting it up I saw it was all gummy and I thought the man was probably dead." He went next door and found Charlotte Anderson, Minor's common-law wife, and "to me she appeared to have been badly beaten, her face was swollen, very badly bruised." He told Charlotte that Minor was shot, and her friend told him "he should have been shot." Charlotte Anderson had been in the hospital a few days earlier because Minor had beaten her with an iron pipe, and because she remained in pain, she begged him to take her back. Minor refused, telling her, "Oh, bitch, go on suffering and die." "She told me," McBride reported, "that when he came home . . . he sat upon the bed and she placed the shotgun against his back and fired one shot." The court was lenient with Anderson despite obvious premeditation, finding her guilty of manslaughter and sentencing her to two to three years' imprisonment.[50] The involvement of seventeen African American women in domestic homicides (by comparison, white women appeared as defendants in only three cases in my sample, and two were infanticides) suggests the pressures placed on black unions. A history of black female wage earning gave women comparative independence from their mates, likely exacerbated male feelings of inadequacy, and heightened tensions between partners that sometimes exploded into homicide.

Women involved in nondomestic homicides acted in ways and for reasons very similar to men. Drunken brawls, jealousy, petty arguments, and involvement in the vice trade all led women to homicide. Peggy Lloyd dumped oil on Pepper Berry and set her ablaze after the two housemates had a quarrel about whether or not Berry should go out for more booze.[51] Erseline Carter killed James Matt, who was affected by paralysis, after a round of drinking in his apartment. Matt threatened to shoot his nephew, Carter asked to see the gun, and the two argued over whether or not Matt would shoot someone—a foolish challenge to a paralyzed man's vulnerable sense of masculinity. Matt said he should kill her, reached over and cut Carter on the thigh, and Carter grabbed a knife and stabbed him in the chest.[52] Beulah Perry and her sister Sadie Washington decided to rob a john and hailed a man passing in the street below, who came upstairs. While one had sex with him, the other stole his wallet. When he protested, their housemate Charles Armstead intervened and hit the man in the head with a hammer and killed him. Perry and Washington fled, and Armstead hid the body in the outhouse, later tossing it over the fence into the vacant lot where it was found.[53] Both domestic and nondomestic homicides were the actions of women fending for themselves in a social setting where the intemperate use of violence supported claims of male dominance—and conversely of female resistance.

Felony homicides (that is, a homicide occurring during the commission of another felony) were relatively rare (6.6 percent). These were almost always "economic" crimes—in the sense that robbery was the motive—and the most common scenario was a holdup in which a shopkeeper resisted his robbers and was killed. Since shopkeepers were frequently white, these homicides made front-page news and prosecutors treated them as hot-button political cases where a first-degree murder conviction made the defendant eligible for the death penalty.[54] A series of robberies of North Philadelphia stores by two holdup men led police to stake out a grocery store at 18th and Berks. The officers were hidden in the back when two robbers came into the store near closing time, and while one opened the cash register, the other ushered the owner, Benjamin Kahn, to the back of the store at gunpoint. Kahn dove for the floor and called out for help, and in an exchange of gunfire, one of the police officers, George Mitchell, was killed. Both holdup men got away, but twenty-three-year-old Theodore Elliott and his twenty-four-year-old cousin, John Frank, were soon arrested. Pressure to convict was intense, and the police moved Elliott from police station to police station, keeping him from his family and allegedly without food until he signed a confession.[55] Kahn was a weak witness, admitting he had failed to pick out either man in police lineups, though on the stand he definitively identified Elliott as the triggerman. Each of the robbers claimed the other was the shooter, although Frank, an admitted heroin addict, stated believably, "When we go in on a holdup, I am a little nervous with a gun, so Elliott always takes the gun and he marches the people back. I go for the money. I usually go over the counter." Elliott subsequently withdrew his not-guilty plea, and a three-judge panel sentenced him to death, while Frank was given life imprisonment.[56] The prominence of cases with white victims, the prosecutor's request for the death penalty, and frequent allegations of police misconduct and beatings likely solidified beliefs among African Americans that the criminal justice system was not to be relied on as it was biased and meted out more punishment than justice to black defendants.

Interracial homicides, such as the murder of Officer Mitchell, occurred rarely—only a dozen cases (7 percent) in my sample over the decade—but it is notable that only one occurred before 1944. That year the Philadelphia Transportation Company's white workers walked off their jobs to protest hiring black motormen and conductors, effectively shutting down the city's war production efforts through their strike. Only federal intervention forced workers back to their jobs amid noticeably increased racial tension in the city.[57] The interracial homicides that appeared during and after 1944 were a mixed lot, however: a black cabbie who killed one of a group of white teenagers in a wild melee that swirled around the dispatch station was acquitted;[58] a white bartender shot a black patron who threatened him with a knife and was acquitted, even though it appeared he chased the fleeing man up the street firing a pistol;[59] a white longshoreman was acquitted of killing a black longshoreman in a street fight involving several men swinging baling hooks and knives. Both the defendant and the deceased had arrest records, and the jury did not want to convict a white man in a brawl among thugs.[60]

The increase in interracial homicides, even though their number remained small, reflected the divisions in a city where race was contested at nearly every turn. The series of acquittals made it seem as if juries decided that the racial contest for the streets was best settled there rather than in court, an ominous portent for a city experiencing wrenching social change.[61] The failure of authorities to act more forcefully in interracial incidents underscored the prevailing view among African Americans that self-reliance was the best protection when venturing in inner-city streets.

Homicide in the postwar city had distinctive racial, gender, and social patterns. The character of most homicides—the brutal, messy confrontations between friends and the violent abuse of spouses—was based in a precarious masculinity that had few supports other than violent self-representation in the ghettoizing city. In the absence of community safeguards against violence and without trusted authorities to intervene, violent men and women responded to the social insecurities of ghetto life by acting collectively in such a way that ensured further violence.

Homicide rates for African Americans and for whites declined in the mid-1950s (Figure 1). The trauma of postwar readjustments in marital relationships that helped cause homicide to spike in 1945–46 ended, and family formation in the 1950s helped bring homicide rates down. The anticipated postwar recession did not occur, and the city enjoyed a modest, if temporary, prosperity. African Americans greeted the opening of public housing projects that replaced some of the city's worst dwellings in North Philadelphia with enthusiasm—until it became apparent that patterns of segregation were (literally) being cemented in the city.[62] A new liberal Democratic city administration promised reform and renewal, although these hopes were eventually dashed.[63]

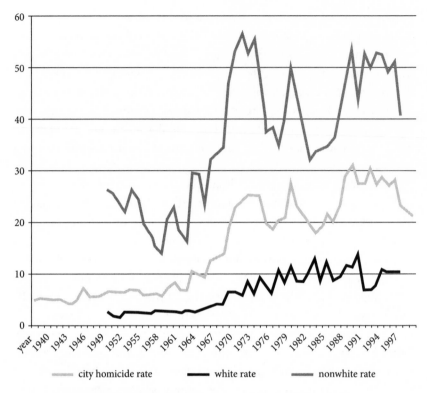

Figure 1. Philadelphia Homicide Rates, per 100,000 Population, 1938–2000.
Source: Philadelphia Department of Public Health, Annual Reports,
1938–2000.

The respite from homicide was relatively brief. As Philadelphia's black
neighborhoods expanded and consolidated, as white ethnic enclaves
resisted the expansion of black settlement, as construction and other unions
rejected NAACP demands for integrated training programs and battled
picketers in the street, as schools became vehicles for miseducation, as factories closed and buildings were left for arsonists, as the drug economy
replaced the mainstream one, as police meted out street justice and the
courts prescribed ever-longer prison sentences, and as poverty concentrated
in spatially isolated communities, ghettoization proceeded apace. As it did,
so did black homicide.

## Chapter 2

# Killing Women and Women Who Kill

## Intimate Homicides

Postwar Philadelphia exhibited what criminologists call a "traditional" pattern of homicide: victims and perpetrators knew each other because of either friendship or familial bonds, and acquaintance, family, and intimate partner homicides together accounted for two-thirds of all murders.[1] In addition, homicide statistics displayed distinctive racial and gender patterns, as both white men and women had low victimization rates while African American men and women were dramatically overrepresented as murder perpetrators and victims.[2] In fact, homicides of and by African American males were the driving force behind the city's homicide rate in this period and beyond.

The acquaintance homicides that predominated among African American men can be explained by the environment of social insecurity in which most African Americans lived. African Americans were simultaneously overpoliced and underpoliced: police stopped and searched young men and moved them off street corners while simultaneously downplaying or ignoring black-on-black crime.[3] Men venturing into public spaces, including taverns ("taprooms"), dance halls, juke joints, and gambling spots, knew they could not rely on police for security, and therefore they carried the means of their own self-defense.[4] High unemployment left time for loitering on street corners and drinking with friends, which fueled and provided the audience for conflict. Individually rational behavior—carrying a weapon—produced collective insecurity and high homicide rates, as any confrontation had the possibility of turning lethal.[5]

That men were prepared to use weapons also escalated the potential for violence with their lovers, spouses, and relatives. The need to assert dominance, a touchy sense of honor, and a masculinity that depended on sexual possessiveness and control have all been identified by scholars as sources of domestic violence.[6] This was nowhere more apparent than in the domestic homicide cases among African Americans, where about a quarter of all the murders committed by black men were of their intimate partners. African American women, who were more likely than white men to be victims and perpetrators of murder, also resorted to weapons in lethal confrontations with their partners, who accounted for nearly two-thirds of African American women's murder victims. That many of women's intimate partner murders were "victim precipitated"—that is, the incidents began in violent actions taken by the eventual victim—again points to the crucial role played by African American men in murder.[7]

All forms of homicide increased suddenly after World War II, and both the nation and Philadelphia were jarred by the increase, especially after unprecedented low rates in the war years.[8] Homicide rates then declined in the late 1940s and remained relatively stable for nearly a decade before starting a steady upward trend toward the end of the 1950s. Intimate partner homicides displayed an inconsistent relationship to the overall homicide rate at least in terms of how cases were prosecuted, but over time domestic murders remained a major contributor to homicide in the city.[9] The accounts of two returning World War II veterans charged with murdering their wives illustrate issues of time, race, and gender in intimate partner homicide.[10]

Lieutenant Howard Brock returned to his North Philadelphia home on Easter Sunday, 1946, after three years' deployment in Europe. Expecting to find his wife, May, Brock rang the doorbell only to discover that she had rented out the house, sold the furniture, given away his clothes, and disappeared with the contents of their savings account. Brock went to see his in-laws in New Jersey, but they claimed to have no knowledge of their daughter's whereabouts. Despite hearing from his sister that she had seen May on the arm of another man downtown, Brock remained determined to reunite with his wife, and he returned to living with his parents in Philadelphia while he continued to search for her.

Finally, after several months May contacted Howard at the request of her parents. The pair arranged to meet at a cafeteria in downtown Philadelphia, and Howard begged her to come back. "I said, 'Please won't you come back to me? . . . My wife started to cry. I was holding her hand.'" But May said she did not love him and no longer wished to live with him. As a ploy to escape her husband, May agreed to think things over and to let him know in a couple of days. The result was predictable: May wrote him a letter saying, "When I saw you Saturday my answer was no. I didn't have to think it over as my mind was made up a long time. So the answer is still no. Do not come up or try to see me as we have nothing more to talk over."

Despite the seeming finality of May's answer, Brock did not give up. He drove the streets of Philadelphia looking for his wife, showing her photograph around and going to the police as well as Legal Aid for help. Then one night he happened to see her in a line of patrons entering a restaurant. Brock parked his car, waited for her to leave, and then tailed her to the White House Hotel where she was staying. He cased the hotel for two days before deciding to wait for her on the porch one night. When he met her there, she was obviously startled but agreed to let him come up to her room so they could speak in private. There they had intercourse, and Brock maintained that May had declared her love for him and agreed to reconcile, though he later admitted showing her a gun that he had in his briefcase, which no doubt intimidated her. The couple headed to a nearby restaurant to celebrate and plan for the future. However, after dinner May suddenly pushed Howard's arm away and told him that she wanted to "be in the single stage." Brock responded,

> I said, "You want to be in the single stage? What do you mean?"
> I said, "What is the meaning of this?"
> She said, "I don't love you."
> I said, "Don't love me?" I said, "Upstairs you told me you loved me, and you told me you loved me down here, and now you tell me you don't love me."
> She said, "Well, I don't love you now. That is all there is to it."

Brock turned ashen and pulled a commando knife from his pocket as his screaming wife fled up Broad Street. Brock tackled her and stabbed her eleven times before burying the knife to its hilt in her heart. Brock collapsed insensibly across his dead wife's body. A night watchman, who witnessed the murder and fired warning shots in the air to summon police, said Brock was "completely out" and picking him up was "just like lifting a sack."

While Brock's murderous assault made front-page news, Grover Richards's murder of his wife a few months earlier went unnoticed. Richards returned from service in the South Pacific in December 1945 and went to live with his wife and mother-in-law. Unlike the Brocks, who apparently had an amicable relationship before the war, Grover and his wife, Doris, had separated, and their problems reemerged on Grover's return. For one thing, Grover wanted Doris to quit her job. "I said her job was coming in between our happiness, where she would have to stay at home with the kids," but Doris, used to the independence supplied by her job, refused to surrender to Grover's patriarchal domestic dreams. "So we just got along, but all the time she got colder toward me, and we could not hardly make out," Grover recalled. It did not help matters when Grover found love letters from another man, Clarence Toomer, stashed in a bureau. "Hello Sweet hart," Toomer wrote, "how are you today fine I hope I am fine I am sitting down looking at your picture this morning I kiss it about 10 times I can't forget about the time I were kissing you. I told you you have the sweetest Lips I ever Kiss. I only wish I were with you . . . it will make me feel much better if I just could hear from you."

Toomer had even been visiting the house the day Richards first returned to Philadelphia, but Richards claimed not to be bothered about the affair. "I told her there is no use fussing and arguing or anything about it, about what you have done since I have been gone, I don't care about that, all I know is I am back and I want some happiness." But happiness was not Grover Richards's fate, and Ella Bell, Doris's mother, recalled Grover saying ominously, "If I can't live with you, nobody else is."

Matters came to a head on February 14, 1946. (Apparently no one noted the possible significance of Valentine's Day in the homicide.) Grover spent the night elsewhere and went back to the house after having several drinks with his father, who ran a bar nearby. Ernest, the couple's six-year-old, wanted doughnuts for breakfast, so Grover turned around and went to the store before heading back upstairs to see his wife. Grover had been thinking about moving out and using the GI Bill to get a home of his own, but Doris was pregnant. Grover maintained, "I didn't want to leave her in that condition." Then Doris dropped the bombshell. "Don't worry about me," she told him, "worry about yourself, it wasn't yours, now give me my key and get the hell out." Instead, Grover pulled out a gun and shot her in the head.

While both Brock and Richards went on trial for first-degree murder (both had earlier acquired guns, suggesting premeditation), the outcomes of their trials were significantly different. Brock, white, college educated, winner of two battle stars, and with a supportive family who helped pay his court expenses, entered a plea of temporary insanity and hired two psychiatrists who testified to the fact. Richards was African American, poor, and had a prior conviction for a violent assault: his father-in-law had pulled a knife when intervening in an argument between Doris and Grover several years earlier, and Grover had shot him. However, both Brock and Richards received what might be called a veteran's discount. One potential juror in Brock's trial explained during *voir dire* what others likely felt: "I don't believe I could convict that man. An ex-G.I. Honestly, I don't believe I could." With even the prosecution's psychiatrist agreeing that Brock had suddenly snapped (despite the evidence of several months of stalking while carrying weapons), the jury found him not guilty of murder. Playing the aggrieved white war hero betrayed by an unfaithful spouse, Brock capitalized on advantages conferred by gender, race, class, and a nation's concern about reintegrating veterans into American society. Other defendants were not so advantaged.

Grover Richards's attorney made an explicit, though not entirely successful, appeal to gender and patriotism. He declared that Richards, winner of a bronze star, had fought "courageously and honorably for . . . [Doris] and for all of us in the hell-holes of the South Pacific Islands," only to return to find "his wife had been prostituting his home." The final indignity, discovering that the child she was carrying was not his, led to this "terribly tragic overpowering moment." The three-judge panel that heard Richards's case was less sympathetic than Brock's jury, but the jurists dismissed the charge of first-degree murder nevertheless and convicted Richards of voluntary manslaughter, choosing to emphasize the confrontation in the bedroom while ignoring the fact that Richards had acquired the gun several days before the shooting. The panel gave Richards a six- to twelve-year sentence but instructed that his war record and Toomer's love letters be forwarded to the parole board for later consideration. Here again, wartime service mitigated the crime without absolving Richards, with his prior record of violence.

Brock's and Richards's cases, except for their outcomes, were typical of male domestic partner homicide. Most defendants, even veterans, were convicted of second-degree murder and given lengthy prison sentences in cases that occurred after the immediate shock of postwar readjustment wore off. Men frequently stalked women from whom they were separated, killed romantic rivals, and murdered from the desire to maintain control over their former partners.

Howard Brock's case, however, was unusually newsworthy, and not just because he was a veteran who committed a gruesome murder on one of the city's major streets. Homicide among whites was extremely rare in postwar Philadelphia and thus made the news when it occurred. The high rates of homicide that had characterized white Philadelphians, especially Irish and Italians, in the nineteenth century, virtually disappeared by the middle of the twentieth century. White Philadelphians sustained a "European" rate of only 1.9 homicide deaths per 100,000 people, and over the entire two decades only 14 percent of the defendants (fifty-three) in all types of homicide were white males.[11] About 20 percent of these cases (eleven) involved an intimate partner, and in a pattern similar to that found in other countries, male defendants in white intimate partner homicides outnumbered female defendants by about three to one. Brock's obsessive pursuit of his wife and the extreme violence he used in killing her were characteristic of 40 percent of the white intimate homicide cases. The remaining partner homicides generally occurred as a result of domestic violence or alcohol abuse, and one killing that took place in the home involving little forethought.[12] The sudden spate of homicides in 1945 and 1946 suggests the difficulties American society faced as veterans and their families adjusted to peacetime. Four of the eleven partner homicides committed by white men between 1940 and 1960 clustered in just these two years, although the small number of cases makes the pattern more suggestive than conclusive. As Dane Archer and Rosemary Gartner have found, there is a correlation between war and homicide that occurs in both victorious and defeated countries, even though veterans are not more prone to homicide than others.[13] The data here suggest that white men in particular had difficulty coming to terms with gender roles that had shifted during the war years as women enjoyed unprecedented levels of employment and consequent economic and social independence.

White women were even less likely than white men to be involved in homicide either as victims or as perpetrators. Of the ten white women tried for homicide in these two decades (less than 3 percent of all defendants), four murdered partners and three of these cases fit the pattern of battered wives killing their husbands in the midst of a murderous assault: in other words, they were "victim-precipitated."[14] Only one case ended in a conviction and jail term. That defendant, Evelyn Newman, plotted with her lover, Wade Horner, to kill her abusive husband, whom the couple buried in the basement after a shooting one night. They then fled Philadelphia for her mother's home in Pittsburgh, and the neighbors discovered the body the next day as they rooted through the cellar looking for coal. Despite ample evidence that Donald Newman had severely neglected his children, beat his wife repeatedly, and threatened to kill her on several occasions, jurors could not ignore the fact that Evelyn Newman's lover shot Donald Newman as he slept. Both parties were found guilty of first-degree murder, with Horner sentenced to die in the electric chair. Although their initial convictions were eventually overturned, both were found guilty of second-degree murder in new trials, and each received a standard ten- to twenty-year prison term.[15] Although "battered spouse syndrome" was not recognized at the time, generally courts took domestic violence into account when adjudicating cases and leveled only modest sentences against defendants or absolved them of guilt when their cases included elements of self-defense.

For African Americans, homicide followed a very different pattern, and Grover Richards's murder of his wife was more representative of murder in the city. African Americans had a homicide victimization rate of 22.5 per 100,000, about eleven times the white rate, and African Americans were defendants in three-quarters of my sample; so the fact that Richards's murder of his wife did not make the news is hardly surprising. Black males were charged in 58 percent of the sampled cases (226), and a quarter of black male defendants (58) killed intimate partners. Black domestic violence was endemic, occurring over the entire period, and not just in a spike after World War II.[16] What accounts for this entrenched violence?

African American Philadelphians encountered a color line in housing, schooling, recreation, and employment that was created by spatial segregation, rampant discrimination, and public policy. Areas of African American settlement consolidated into ghettos that were hemmed in by hostile neighbors and cemented in place by the location of public housing in predominantly black neighborhoods. African American migrants streamed into Philadelphia, helping the city's black population more than double between 1930 and 1960. Southern migrants arrived from the most murder-prone section of the country, where the police were barely distinguishable from white terrorists and where the courts acted to maintain white supremacy. Not surprisingly, southern African Americans brought with them a tradition of self-reliance in handling disputes and a well-grounded mistrust of public authorities, which melded with a similar suspicion, if not hostility, toward police rooted in black Philadelphians' experience.[17] Black men of all backgrounds asserted themselves when and where they could, on neighborhood streets and in their homes, while doing their best to remain beyond the surveillance of public authorities.

In was not insignificant that the violence that occurred in black Philadelphia was steeped in alcohol. "Carry outs" (delis and restaurants that sold beer) and legal and illegal liquor outlets dotted poor neighborhoods and shaped their social environment. Residents kept moonshine ("white whiskey") stills in backyards, neighbors sold liquor by the glass in their kitchens to supplement meager wages, and taprooms occupied many corner locations. Police even established a category of "taproom homicides" to account for the murders (8 percent) that took place either in bars or on nearby street corners.[18] In nearly half of these murders (one-quarter among whites), the defendant, the victim, or both were drunk at the time of the incident, with autopsies sometimes revealing extraordinary blood alcohol levels. Liquor magnified minor insults, lowered inhibitions, and turned disputes deadly while a house full of drinking buddies provided the audience for sparring partners.

Intimate partner homicide was obviously linked to domestic violence, but it also represented an extension of the violence that occurred in African American neighborhoods. Men used knives—pocketknives, gravity knives, and switchblades—in 40 percent of the domestic homicides and guns in 29 percent of them; usually these were the weapons men carried with them when venturing into public space. So, for example, when Charles and Henrietta Speller began arguing over whether or not she had money to buy wine, Henrietta pulled her knife and "up and stabbed me," Charles explained to police. "I reached into my right hand coat pocket and got my knife out and I stabbed her." Speller conceded that he always carried a knife with him, as did his wife: "She never carried any knife of mine. I had my own knife."[19] Leroy Turner went on trial for knifing his common-law wife, Mary Davis, in a drunken brawl. He later explained, "I told Mary she ain't going to sleep with me tonight, I don't want no woman sleeping with me who stayed in the street all the time." Mary in turn accused Leroy of having sex with her mother. As the argument escalated, Mary went downstairs and returned with a butcher knife. "So I reached and got my knife which was . . . in the scabbard," Leroy recounted. "I stabbed her and then walked out of the room."[20] Men carried weapons for safety in the streets but did not necessarily disarm themselves once they returned home. So armed, these men turned assaults into murders.

Because male authority in the home was precarious, the threat of violence became one way of maintaining it. African American women had much higher labor-force participation rates than white women, and as a result, they were used to making decisions, handling money, controlling their leisure time, picking sexual partners, ending relationships, and, when time and energy permitted, enjoying the freedom of the city.[21] Greater parity with their male partners fostered conflict, and minor incidents could set men off as they reacted to challenges, perceived or real. William Jeffrey started cursing his wife, Margaret, because her shoes had touched his pants as he brushed passed her. She went to make his lunch, but "every time I got near him he just glared and rolled his eyes." William had beaten her several times despite her pregnancy, and Margaret had had enough. So she "went into the kitchen and picked up the gun from behind the door and stood in the doorway and started to shoot."[22] In another case, when Penny Fuller's husband, Paul, asked her to get some "goat head" (moonshine), she "told him he didn't need any more to drink." Outraged at being told what to do by his wife, Paul grabbed her and threw her against the wall and kicked her repeatedly in the groin. Penny took a knife from the kitchen table and stabbed Paul to death.[23] And John Snipes killed Mabel Snipes in an argument that started when she made "insulting remarks" about his mother.[24] While all of these seemingly trivial incidents were only the immediate triggers to homicide, the visible surface of hidden conflict, they suggest the prickly nature of male pride. Masculinity depended on meeting challenges. On the street, masculinity was performed before an audience that appraised its success, while in the home it depended on the ability to control the actions of one's intimate partner or to cow her into obedience. Disobedience merited punishment, a reassertion of power (and therefore of self-respect) over an independent partner.

Charges of infidelity were involved in 40 percent of the domestic cases with male defendants, suggesting the fragility of domestic bonds and the sense of masculinity that rested on them. Intimate bonds, whether or not sanctioned by the state, were easily frayed, and men often exploded into violence.[25] Stanley Johnson told police he had ordered his wife out of the Bobo Bar, but she "disobeyed" him. Shortly before closing time, he told her again to go home and again she said no. Johnson left and eventually returned home around 2:30 a.m., "and as I walked in the door, she was in bed with a man." Johnson started to beat her with a wooden board. "I never let up on my anger until I thought it was enough," he said, but by then it was too late.[26]

Nearly a fifth of these murders involved a man killing a male romantic rival. Edward Riley returned home unexpectedly and found the door barred. Pushing it open, he asked "What's going on here?" A man replied, "I'm fucking your wife." Riley got a knife from the kitchen and stuck it in his chest.[27] Such encounters went to the core of a man's identity: could a cuckold be a man at all? Riley's masculinity was diminished by his rival's ability to take possession of his wife and then taunt him about it. Violence redressed the balance.

Catching one's spouse "in the act" may have been a justification for homicide in English common law, but Philadelphia courts extended no such right. Such murders may have occurred in "hot blood," which therefore reduced the culpability of the defendant, but the courts exhibited limited tolerance for naked assertions of male privilege. Defendants found themselves guilty of second-degree murder more frequently than for manslaughter (49 percent vs. 31 percent), while another 16 percent of defendants were found guilty of murder in the first degree. Philadelphia courts—despite the examples of war veterans Brock and Richards—took spousal murder seriously and punished the men who committed it.

While African American women confronted the same environment of social insecurity that men did, and sometimes carried weapons in their pocketbooks, their greatest threats lived at home with them. At a time when domestic violence went unrecognized as a matter for public policy, when women's shelters were nonexistent, and when calls to the police sometimes went unanswered or produced no action, women knew they were largely on their own. Ella Allen, for example, was asked why she did not call police when her husband beat her and replied that when police came, they said, "Oh, it's just family trouble, husband and wife," and told her husband, Walter, to "take a walk around the block."[28] Albert Trimmer, the house sergeant, testified in another case that he sent a "red car" (Philadelphia police car) to the home of Ola and Van Wilson on a few occasions at the request of neighbors to quiet disturbances. But there were no other interventions until Ola stabbed Van to death with an ice pick.[29] The situation in the home replicated the social insecurity of the streets, and women used the weapons they found around the household, taking their partners' handguns, grabbing knives from the kitchen, or loading shotguns to defend themselves.

Women were less likely to kill their husbands in a fight over another woman, and there are no examples of a woman killing another woman over alleged infidelity. Women did not stalk their partners or kill them and other family members in violent retribution for threatened abandonment, and in this, African American women acted similarly to white women.[30] Nellie Hatch's case came closest to the traditional male pattern: she followed her husband, Willie, and Pency Mae Johnson to an apartment, burst through the door, and "saw Pency Mae and my husband lying on a cot with no clothes on . . . having relations with each other." Nellie grabbed a knife from the kitchen and cut Pency Mae on the shoulder before her husband disarmed her and pushed her out the door. Unfortunately for Willie, Nellie went home, got another knife, and, subsequently encountering her husband on the street, stabbed him to death.[31] Even though Hatch had time to cool off, which should have raised her offense to second-degree murder, the court convicted her only of voluntary manslaughter.

When African American women killed men who were abusive, the court usually tempered its judgment and declined to find them guilty of first- or second-degree murder. In two-thirds of the cases, black women defendants were found guilty of voluntary manslaughter and, in another 20 percent, of involuntary manslaughter; 16 percent were adjudged not guilty by reason of self-defense, as judges and juries took a history of difficult relationships into account. When Charlotte Anderson, for example, was severely beaten with a lead pipe, Sam Minor, her common-law husband, refused to take her to the hospital, so a neighbor bundled her into a cab ("she couldn't hardly walk") and took her to the emergency room. The doctor treated her and told her to come back the next day for X-rays, but again Sam would not take her. Assuming no responsibility for his actions, he declared that she was getting on his nerves with all her moaning and whimpering. He said, "I'm going to get this iron pipe and kill you" before heading out the door. Anderson told police that she took his shotgun out of the closet and placed it on a chair next to the bed. When he returned home and sat on the bed, she reached for the shotgun and killed him. At her trial Charlotte changed her story and claimed that Sam was coming toward her with the pipe when she shot him, making a case for self-defense rather than the premeditated murder that appeared to have occurred. The court, swayed by Sam Minor's history of brutality and by police testimony of how badly beaten Charlotte was, found her guilty of voluntary manslaughter and recommended a relatively light twenty-four- to thirty-six-month sentence.[32]

As these accounts suggest, African American women such as Charlotte Anderson had almost an equal chance of being on the witness stand as on the coroner's slab. In the survey of intimate partner homicides among African Americans, women accounted for over 40 percent of the murders. African Americans were the only group in which males did not outnumber female defendants by three or four to one. This contrasts sharply with both white American and European patterns of intimate partner homicide. The contemporary scholarly literature that discusses domestic homicide in terms of female victimization and "learned helplessness" is much more applicable to white domestic homicide than it is to African American homicide.[33] For African American women, as for African American men, there was no dichotomy between "home" and "street," as the environment of social insecurity shaped both, and in the case of abusive partners, women acted to preserve themselves even if judges and juries did not always see their actions as self-defense.

As the cases of Howard Brock and Grover Richards suggest, whites and blacks exhibited distinctive patterns of intimate partner homicide in postwar Philadelphia that reflected the distinctly different social environments they inhabited. Among whites, public order and high rates of industrial employment kept homicide rates low well into the postwar period, and domestic homicide was no exception. Most white males who killed their female partners did so in fits of jealous rage, while women rarely initiated lethal violence even in very abusive relationships. Homicide was the result more of individual than social circumstance.

By contrast, in African American neighborhoods marked by segregation, discrimination, and public neglect, violence was endemic, and it seeped into the home as well. Male murderers were a majority in cases of domestic homicide, and they killed their partners in an effort to maintain masculine identities through the assertion of power and control. But African American women took the initiative to kill abusive partners with relative frequency. Women, used to negotiating a dangerous public space and aware that public authorities would do little to help them, exhibited self-reliance, carried weapons, and used violence in ways similar to African American men in the public space. An environment of social insecurity shaped the behaviors of both African American men and women, and collectively they generated high levels of murder. In the process, they both produced and were entangled in a self-perpetuating homicidal environment that continues to haunt the modern city.

*Chapter 3*

# Race and Murder in the Remaking of West Philadelphia

Race, murder, and urban renewal are inextricably linked to the history of West Philadelphia from the 1950s to the present.[1] Yet discussions of urban renewal in Philadelphia—and elsewhere—pay little or no attention to the effect of violent crime on redevelopment practice. Nor have criminologists taken up crime's ecological context to analyze how it has prompted changes in the physical and social environment.[2] While it is well-known that urban universities used renewal funds to stabilize adjacent residential areas in the face of racial change, to expand outdated campus facilities, to unify and beautify campus landscapes, to assert their institutional primacy in the local economy, and to create sites for science and technology start-ups,[3] the effect of violent crime on those decisions has been largely ignored.[4] In 1958, the killing of University of Pennsylvania graduate student In-Ho Oh by a group of African American adolescents exposed racial fault lines in the city and galvanized the University of Pennsylvania and a consortium of local institutions to form the West Philadelphia Corporation to clear the Black Bottom neighborhood for a university-related science center in order to create a *cordon sanitaire* just north of campus. In yet another fashion, murder and the reactions to it provide a window into the history of the postwar city.

On the evening of April 25, 1958, small groups of teenaged boys gathered in the Powelton Village streets near the Penn campus, some intending to go to a dance sponsored by a local church, while others just milled around enjoying the seasonably mild spring evening. Although Powelton was an integrated community with a progressive reputation, most of the boys were drawn from other nearby African American neighborhoods that were intensely poor, overcrowded, and filled with recent arrivals, many from the South, who were funneled into West Philadelphia's oldest and most rundown areas.[5]

While most of the teens filed peacefully into the St. Andrew's Church auditorium, a small group remained outside the vestry door. W. W. Lorick, who ran the Friday-night dances for the neighborhood teens, recalled that "some boys came up, and they asked to—could they come in. I told them no, because they didn't live around there, and some of the boys had been drinking, and so I had to refuse them from the door." One of the boys claimed that if he got the thirty-five cents admission fee, "one way or another, we are going to get in here." The group then shouted some expletives, and one of the volunteers called the police. By the time police arrived, the group had left the church, and the dance went on peacefully.

Another teen, Alfonso "Flip" Borum, came to the door and was admitted by asking for one of the volunteers by name. When asked for his membership card, however, he said, "I don't have a card. You know me, Mr. Montague." Montague testified, "When he called my name, I recognized him. He had dark glasses on and he pulled his glasses off. I said, 'That's the rule. That goes for you or anybody else,' and he went out."

Flip Borum and the other youths continued to mill around in the neighborhood. A student from nearby Drexel Institute contacted a private security guard, who patrolled the streets near the fraternity houses that dotted the area, about the presence of a boisterous group of teens on the street. After questioning the youths, the guard ordered them to keep moving. A neighbor, getting off the bus to return to her home, recalled that the teens were running, hollering, and carrying on. She went to a friend's house and asked to call the police "because I thought these boys were acting in a very ugly manner." And their manner was about to get uglier.[6]

In-Ho Oh, twenty-six years old, who at the time of his death was a graduate student in political science at the University of Pennsylvania, came to the United States in 1957 as an exchange student to East Baptist College from Seoul Korean National University. Oh, like many members of his family, was a Christian and had strong ties to the United States, with six family members who had studied here. He had also served as an interpreter for the U.S. Army during the Korean War and went on to study international politics after completing his undergraduate theological studies. Oh, who lived with his aunt and uncle, had just finished writing a letter to his family in Korea and decided to go around the corner to a nearby postal box to mail it.[7]

Oh mailed his letter and was crossing the street to return to his apartment when three of the teens decided to mug him. Douglas Clark, fifteen years old; Robert Williams, seventeen; and Percy Johnson, seventeen, grabbed Oh and started punching him, but Oh struggled free and ran into the street.[8] Sixteen-year-old Franklin Marshall and Leonard Johnson, fifteen, joined in the chase, and Clark tripped Oh as he was trying to get away. "'I stuck out my foot to trip him but he stumbled,' Clark testified. 'I did it only for a gag.'"[9] Leonard Johnson, who had said earlier "he was tired doing all this walking for nothing, that he was going to get somebody with his blackjack," now had his chance.

Another boy recounted, "I seen Franklin Marshall with one arm around the man hitting him. He hollered, 'Flip, I need help.' So Alfonso Borum, Lenny Johnson, Harry McCloud, Sonny [Edward] McCloud, and Percy Johnson and James Wright and Douglas Clark—they all ran back to where the scene was happening at. So Alfonso Borum, he hit the man and the man went down. I saw Lenny Johnson hit the man three times with the blackjack."[10] Lenny Johnson later explained his actions by saying, "Well . . . they were all yelling 'hit him, hit him,' so I did."[11] Edward McCloud, who later became a prosecution witness, said, "I heard Flip say, 'Damn, I got blood all over me.' And then he started kicking him like crazy."[12] Another witness claimed, "Then somebody hollered 'get his wallet.' Frank and the boy I don't know looked in his pockets, and then Frank said 'it's not here.' Then the man made a gruntin noise, like a moan, and then Frank said 'shut the fuck up,' and Frank kicked him two times in the face and then everybody just fled."[13] A trail of blood in the street indicated that Oh's body had been dragged for about twelve feet, and a homicide detective later testified that Oh's face was battered beyond recognition with "indentations and depression in the face caused by the kicking and the blows of the blackjack and lead pipe."[14] Blood, bone, and brains oozed out onto the street. The response to the murder was immediate and visceral.

In-Ho Oh's death made national and international news, not only because of the brutality of the attack and the fact that Oh was a Korean citizen, but also because interracial homicide was relatively rare and because of the number of his youthful attackers. In a pattern typical of homicide generally, less than 10 percent of all Philadelphia murders involved people of different racial backgrounds.[15] However, interracial homicides made up for the small number with sensational headlines, especially when the perpetrators were black, and Oh's murder certainly fit the bill. Moreover, in this classic era of teenage fighting gangs, the number of assailants immediately led the police and the media to conclude that they were members of a gang, even though there was no evidence beyond the fact that the teens knew each other, as most were students at Overbrook High School. The simple fact that a group of eleven teens was involved invoked the trope of the "street gang murder" as a convenient way of interpreting Oh's killing.[16] Oh's murder did follow what the *Philadelphia Inquirer* called the "continuing wave of hold-ups and attacks" in the West Philadelphia area, most of which were perpetrated by young men.[17] The city seemed besieged by gang violence and youthful predators.

The defendants themselves did little to help their case. No doubt bewildered by the press and public attention and either unaware of or shrinking from the enormity of their deed, the youths postured and acted out both in public and in jail. They giggled and clowned before the judge at their arraignment, and once in the lockup, they shouted boisterously and "jostled each other, told off-color stories, shouted, screamed and danced around" until they were moved into separate cells. Such bravado was quite common in criminal cases involving juveniles, who were sometimes goaded by journalists into acting out before the cameras: this was a chance to act "bad" and preen before the public, and the attention from onlookers, the media, the police, and court officials verified the self, proved one's manliness, and stoked one's image back in the neighborhood.[18]

Within days, the teens' juvenile records were made public. Most of their offenses were minor but not all. Franklin Marshall had been arrested four times, including once for a gang fight that involved a stabbing; Edward McCloud, Harry McCloud, and Harold Johnson all had burglary arrests, while Lonnie Collins was part of a group allegedly responsible for fifty muggings and had been on probation twice for aggravated assault and battery. Borum had recently been paroled from White Hill Reform School, where he had served time for statutory rape and general delinquency, while Percy

Johnson was awaiting trial for extortion.[19] These were youths familiar to police and familiar with the processes of criminal justice, but none had served any length of time for their previous criminal actions.

The young men's seemingly brazen attitude, their juvenile records of arrests followed by what some considered "coddling" in the juvenile justice system, together with the crime itself, outraged Philadelphians. When the eleven adolescents charged in Oh's murder were arraigned in juvenile court, Judge J. Stanley Hoffman referred to them as "vermin" whose "barbaric piece of savagery" "brought undeserved shame to a decent, law-abiding segment of our population" as he bound them over to be tried in adult court. Editorials in the city papers echoed similar language, using jungle and animal analogies in their descriptions of the youths. "Creatures capable of such a slaying," intoned the *Philadelphia Evening Bulletin*, "could be expected to regard it as insensitively as a pack of hyenas regards a carcass." With District Attorney Victor Blanc calling for the death penalty for all eleven defendants, the hue and cry was just beginning.[20]

Proving a first-degree murder charge against the defendants was not going to be easy, however. The crux of the matter was robbery: if the prosecution could prove that Oh's murder took place as a result of a decision to rob him (hence the testimony about the teens not having the admission price to a dance), then this was a murder occurring during the commission of a felony. Under Pennsylvania law, this automatically raised the murder from second to first degree and made the accused eligible for the death penalty. If, on the other hand, the defendants acted on impulse, with the robbery occurring as an afterthought, then a second-degree murder charge was more sustainable, even given the brutality of the murder. There was also the matter of the defendants' youth to consider; they ranged in age from fifteen to eighteen, and despite Judge Hoffman's decision to have them tried as adults, it was not clear that a jury would impose the death penalty on any one of them, never mind on all. District Attorney Blanc's endorsement of the death penalty for the eleven was more an issue of politics than of law, and Blanc clearly had decided to stoke the flame of public indignation.

As suggested by frequent references to the jungle, the reaction to the murder was imbued with overtones of race as much as with concerns about delinquency. The *Inquirer* declared that African American leaders had a "special responsibility" to fight the high rate of "Negro crime," while a columnist from the city's conservative paper of record, the *Philadelphia Evening Bulletin,* declared bluntly, "Much of the trouble goes back to the younger generation of the Negro race" as he linked the city's loss of population to the suburbs to white fears of the growing "crime wave."[21]

Letters—three boxes worth—poured into Mayor Richardson Dilworth's office following Oh's murder, as Philadelphians registered their fear, outrage, and sense of loss, as well as their suggestions for handling the defendants. The letters revealed a larger sense of displacement as whites and blacks competed for urban space. "I've always loved living in the City of Philadelphia, but during the past year I've thought more than once of moving as far out as possible," stated Marilyn Steinberg. "I'm a working girl and a housewife, hoping to be a mother some day, and I'm not sure I would want my children raised in a community where one walks in fear," she wrote in a comment echoed by many others.[22] Attorney David Malis wrote that he had moved his family from West Philadelphia because "when nightfall came we feared to open the doors and go out of the house."[23] A Mrs. Rafferty complained, "When we lived down in the city . . . it was just one break in after another. . . . No one is fit to walk the streets at night, even during the daytime there have been holdups, pocketbook snatchings, etc."[24] Although many of the letters dripped with racism, the mayor's correspondents cited specific incidents in which they or a family member had been assaulted, held up, burgled, or harassed, nearly always by African American teenagers. "I belong to Jewish War Veterans," one Philadelphia resident wrote. "I'm afraid to go to the meetings, because about 6 months ago I was held up on my own doorstep by a boy of 13."[25] Another resident, the father of three young children, wrote, "I for one don't let my wife go out at evenings but as at present she is working at nite [*sic*] but I go to meet her. This shouldn't be we agree."[26] Suggestions for handling delinquents—the electric chair for In-Ho Oh's killers and public lashings for juvenile offenders at a whipping post set up in City Hall ("Give them as many lashes as they deserve for what they did, and more the next time")—contained obvious racial referents, but they were also the hyperbolic comments of people fed up with crime and with what they believed to be the decline of a great city.[27] These comments were racialized—with traits of individuals being ascribed to a racial group—but they also reflected the lived historical experience of the correspondents, namely, that of being criminally victimized, thus underscoring their feelings of displacement from "their" city.

The mayor's correspondents, at least according to the language they used, were white, but the city's African American population also seemed to favor severe punishment for the defendants in the Oh case. The *Philadelphia Tribune*, the city's African American newspaper, surveyed residents and found a consensus that the eleven youths should be tried as adults and, if found responsible for the killing, should face long jail sentences at a minimum. A handful of respondents favored the death penalty, one supported the idea of installing a whipping post in City Hall, and a number agreed that the justice system was too lenient in its treatment of delinquents. In these sentiments, at least, black Philadelphians did not diverge much from whites. Of course, the *Tribune* was the mouthpiece of established black Philadelphia—the "OPs," or Old Philadelphians, who sometimes looked askance at the countrified migrants who were flocking to the city—and it might be expected to take a more conservative position on law and order. In an editorial reflecting on two additional interracial attacks by youths after the In-Ho Oh murder—one attack on another international student at Penn, the other on an elderly man who died following a beating—the *Tribune* declared, "We think it is going too far to continue the defense of these adult-minded juveniles by saying they are the products of the society that made them what they are." The "vermin" that infest tenements are also a product of society, and "these we exterminate."[28] These sentiments cooled as time went on, and the paper as well as its readers came to express outrage at the double standard of justice in the city, where black delinquents were "beasts" and white ones "misguided."[29] But in the immediate aftermath of the Oh killing, even the mother of one of the defendants declared, "If my boy did this, if he helped kill this man . . . he'll have to pay the price."[30]

The anguish caused by Oh's murder was especially apparent in Powelton Village, an island of Quaker liberalism in a sea of poor African American neighbors. Powelton was home to several Quaker-inspired housing cooperatives that pioneered interracial living, and the Powelton Village Development Association (PVDA), formed in 1956, promoted the careful steering of African American residents so as to maintain racial balance in the community, with no apartment building having more than 50 percent black occupancy.[31] Despite these efforts, the PVDA worried that "long years of poor maintenance, plus the continual reminder of slum conditions surrounding Powelton on three sides and the fear of after-dark violence, have been catching up with Powelton owners unusually rapidly this summer, thanks to the In-Ho Oh incident." Although these were the views of community real estate interests concerned about the value of their investments, they were attuned to the murder's repercussions within the Powelton community they served. Among "white collar families," they noted, there was "something akin to panic," and a number indicated a desire to move to a safer area, while real estate owners faced an unusual level of vacancies in the aftermath of the murder.[32] Philadelphia police commissioner Thomas Gibbons said of the forty-six letters he received about the case, most complaining about the lenient treatment afforded juvenile delinquents, forty came from residents near where the murder had occurred. One letter to District Attorney Blanc demanding justice for In-Ho Oh's killers was co-signed by sixteen residents of the Powelton Apartments. Thomas Curran, the letter writer, concluded, "There never was a night for the past few years, when I retired and opened my windows, that I was not awakened by a woman or man screaming after twelve o'clock at night out on Powelton Avenue–35th or 36th Streets. This neighborhood has been terrorized for two years now by several groups of hoodlums—all teenagers."[33] Even in liberal Powelton, residents demanded law and order.

Others in the neighborhood offered more muted and constructive suggestions. In the face of the violence, residents called a community meeting in St. Andrew's Church—the site of the dance on the night of In-Ho Oh's murder. An overflow crowd estimated at six hundred appeared and demanded more police protection, especially foot patrols; better lighting on the neighborhood's tree-lined streets; zoning code enforcement (to prevent illegal conversions from single-family into multifamily homes); and improved recreational facilities for young people in West Philadelphia. One response to the community meeting came a few nights later when a group, reportedly teenaged friends of the In-Ho Oh defendants, ransacked the offices of the PVDA. Residents tried to calm fears by noting that violent attacks could occur anywhere, not just in their community. By the fall, Powelton leaders expressed confidence that their social experiment in integrated living, though frayed by the murder, remained intact.[34]

Richardson Dilworth also attempted a progressive response to the city's crisis. Unlike in New York City, where public officials deliberately played down the role of race in violent incidents and argued that perpetrators were young psychopaths,[35] Mayor Dilworth addressed the issue of race forthrightly. The patrician mayor was part of a group of liberal Democrats who had campaigned for over a decade on a platform of political reform, urban renewal, and civil rights, including the creation of a city fair-employment practices committee, and they finally succeeded in overthrowing a corrupt Republican machine that had run the city for decades. The Democrats relied on support from a group of white Protestant business leaders, middle-class good-government reformers, and a New Deal coalition of union members, Jews, and African Americans that the crime issue (as much as battles over open housing and civil rights legislation) threatened to fracture.[36] Perhaps because of his strong beliefs and his credentials as a supporter of civil rights, Dilworth thought he could afford to address issues of crime, race, and inequality in a way that other big-city mayors could not.

Dilworth appeared on local television, declaring there "is greater antagonism between the white and Negro communities today in Philadelphia than at any time in the last thirty years."[37] In an effort to contextualize violent crime, he argued that all cities were suffering from an increase in crime and that the incidence of crime in low-income African American neighborhoods was no worse than that in low-income white areas. "The reason the over-all Negro crime percentage is high," Dilworth maintained, "is that there are so many low income Negro districts." Resisting suggestions for repressive punishment by arguing that it was only "counter violence" and unlikely to be effective, the mayor forcibly rejected the notion that segregation made for less crime and better race relations. Instead, he called for traditional progressive remedies: additional social services, more recreational opportunities, and new specialized institutions for juvenile offenders. Moreover, Dilworth blamed whites for discrimination, noting, " 'I do see signs of the Negro in the big city being exploited by landlords, shopkeepers and being kept out of many opportunities they should have." But African Americans did not get off scot-free: the mayor called on them to exhibit more leadership in confronting social problems in their own community. "They can't keep on blaming the whites for all their troubles," Dilworth asserted as he called on all Philadelphians to work together. "Until we regard ourselves as one community, we won't be able to solve the problem."[38]

This stance by the tough former Marine and ex-litigator was characteristically blunt and guaranteed to please no one: too coolly academic in its analysis of crime to appease his white constituents ("I voted for you, may God forgive me,"[39] wrote one woman) and too focused on individual responsibility to appeal to his black ones. Indeed, his speech reveals the difficulty of bridging the racial gap in the increasingly divided postwar city. Dilworth failed to connect his vision of the city—one shared broadly with other postwar urban political regimes that emphasized a revitalized downtown core, the construction of modern housing to lure middle-class whites back from the suburbs, and the creation of a network of limited-access roadways designed to speed motorists between metropolitan destinations— with worsening race relations in the city.[40] Postwar reconstruction projects of the kind being promoted in Philadelphia seemed to offer no place for the poor as they shuffled older and declining communities around, placing African Americans and working-class whites into direct competition for scarce urban space. As the Mayor's Commission on Human Relations declared, the effect of downtown renewal projects "is to push the Negro and lower income population back a few blocks, and to compress it further" as they encountered the boundaries of nearby white communities.[41] Dilworth's policies of modernizing and spatially reorganizing the city undermined directly any broad appeals he made to citizenship, community, and social responsibility.

Dilworth, who had declared famously that suburbanization was creating a "white noose" around Philadelphia and who urged white families to remain in the city, now failed to find the right tone to bring his city together. Speaking at In-Ho Oh's funeral at Old Pine Church, where he called Oh's killing a "terrible, dreadful" thing that made him "ashamed of my city," he broke down in tears. Unable to continue, the emotional Dilworth appeared as deeply concerned for the state of his city as for the unfortunate young man.[42]

If the immediate reaction to Oh's murder involved both racial virulence and soul searching on the part of Philadelphians, the long-term response was more complicated. The problems posed by delinquency and by adolescent street gangs were hardly new, and social work and outreach by community organizations was well established in the city. Moreover, plans for campus expansion and urban renewal had been on the table for over a decade. But Oh's killing crystallized those plans and gave impetus to efforts to remake West Philadelphia and its inhabitants. In that section of the city at least, concerns about violent crime gave urban renewal efforts a certain immediacy and spurred them on as much as the perceptions of blight, racial transition, or the economic malaise of the postwar city had been able to do.

The University of Pennsylvania had been eyeing the areas immediately adjacent to its campus for some time. Future Penn president and prominent urbanist Martin Meyerson wrote the School of Fine Arts dean (and chairman of the Philadelphia City Planning Commission) G. Holmes Perkins in 1956 that "only a vigorous program of planning, redevelopment and rehabilitation of a large area will prevent West Philadelphia from becoming a sea of residential slums with commercial and institutional islands."[43] The expansion of the university's physical plant was an integral part of its ambition to become a world-class research university, attract federal research and development dollars, lure the best faculty and graduate students, and rise above its status as a commuting school bisected by trolley lines and city streets. The so-called Martin Plan, adopted by university trustees in 1948, guided expansion over the next quarter-century by focusing largely on extending the campus's spine westward along Locust Street, with the goal of landscaping it and closing it to vehicular traffic and incorporating adjacent parcels into a unified campus. Penn's incestuous relationship with both the City Planning Commission and the Redevelopment Authority, where both Perkins and Meyerson were members of the Development Committee, meant that the university could expect maximum cooperation from relevant city authorities.[44]

These plans for Penn's expansion aroused little community opposition at first. Absentee owners, who served a student clientele, and speculators, whose interests were primarily economic, owned many of the properties near the university; with Penn paying a fair market price, the owners generally surrendered the properties without objection.[45] A combination of city, state, and federal monies helped Penn acquire, condemn, and clear the land for its expansion and campus beautification. But plans for a "University City" went far beyond the campus proper to encompass a more ambitious remaking of neighborhoods and people.

Within a month of In-Ho Oh's death, University of Pennsylvania trustees approved a new partnership between the university and the Redevelopment Authority to create a "University City."[46] In its earliest iteration, the university agreed simply to acquire and clear adjacent land for which it had no immediate use (in other words, it proposed to engage in land-banking) as part of a "civic betterment" project that would encourage faculty and students to live in new residential quarters near the campus. Some six months later, in January 1959, Penn agreed to partner with the Drexel Institute (later Drexel University), the Philadelphia College of Pharmacy and Science, Presbyterian Hospital, and the Philadelphia College of Osteopathy to form the West Philadelphia Corporation (WPC) as a real estate development entity that was formally independent of its institutional parents.[47] Although Penn dominated the WPC and hired its director, who reported to Penn president Gaylord Harnwell, the WPC's independent status buffered the university from criticism that it was directly involved in clearing land and evicting tenants. The hands of the WPC reached into several communities in West Philadelphia, supporting the creation of community associations in middle-class neighborhoods, championing the interests of faculty who moved there, providing support for local public schools, and supplying funding for housing rehabilitation, but it was in the so-called Black Bottom where its grip was felt most directly.

The Black Bottom—officially Unit III of the West Philadelphia Redevelopment Plan—was a largely, though not exclusively, African American area that lay between the university and Powelton Village. Named the Bottom because of its geographic location along a slope that curved gently upward as one headed west from the Schuylkill River toward Powelton, it was composed of Philadelphia's characteristic two- and three-story row homes as well as some institutional, commercial, and industrial sites. It was also home to the notorious Bottoms gangs, an amalgam of rival groups that united against outside threats and that feuded with the nearby Tops, a similar collective of gangs who resided farther west on "top" of the ridge. Over about a fifteen-year period, the rival teenaged gangs were responsible for at least three murders and several nonfatal shootings.[48] In an analysis of crime in West Philadelphia, the Bottom ranked second in the seriousness among the areas assessed.[49] Although In-Ho Oh's murder inspired the plan to acquire and clear the area, none of his murderers lived there.

The communities in the immediate vicinity of the university, of which the Bottom was a part, underwent a rapid racial transition between 1950 and 1960, with the white population declining by about two-thirds, the "non-white" population nearly doubling, and the overall population increasing slightly (about 10 percent).[50] Since no new housing was built, the increase in population was accommodated through overcrowding, and a Health and Welfare Council study noted that the area had the second highest number of zoning variance requests in the city, as single-family homes were subdivided into smaller apartments.[51] By 1950 the City Planning Commission had identified the area as blighted and certified it for future redevelopment. Only about a quarter of the units were owner occupied compared with a Philadelphia average of more than 60 percent. As a high-crime, high-poverty area undergoing rapid racial transition, with few established stakeholders and its location near the perimeter of the university, the Bottom was an obvious target for Penn's land-banking scheme. As for the six thousand or so residents in the Bottom, 80 percent of whom were "non-white," they faced eviction into Philadelphia's low-income realty market, where they would have to fend for themselves. Monetary compensation for evictees was limited: tenants either received nothing or only a small amount for "hardship" cases; owners received a "fair market value" for their property but one that was significantly depressed by being in an area long slated for renewal.[52] Nearly 95 percent of those relocated in Philadelphia's urban renewal projects were African American, according to a study by the Philadelphia Housing Association, and they were on average twice as poor as other Philadelphians, with only three in ten finding decent housing after they were "renewed" out of their neighborhoods. Urban renewal, in the view of critics, spread slums, and clearing the Bottom was not only going to worsen the plight of its residents but also increase pressure on other nearby neighborhoods as about two-thirds of those displaced resettled within a mile of their original homes.[53]

In the place of the Bottom residences would rise a new "University City," anchored by the University City Science Center, an ambitious plan for a science and technology incubator that was Penn's and Philadelphia's answer to the economic obsolescence of the industrial city. University research would provide the basis for spin-off companies and foster the emergence of a new knowledge-based economy that would propel Philadelphia into the future.

The Science Center itself, supporters maintained, would employ five thousand workers, with ripple effects increasing that number tenfold. Although the physical plans for the site changed over time, the end result was a land-eating complex of medium-sized buildings that extended for four blocks along Market Street, West Philadelphia's main commercial thoroughfare that connected it to Center City. The adjacent streets, the plan imagined, would fill with new residences for faculty, students, scientists, and technicians from the Science Center.[54]

Opposition to the university's plans built slowly and not very effectively. Powelton Village residents eyed University City warily, as theirs was the community closest to the Bottom, and they feared that evictions would send migrants streaming their way and overrun their carefully managed effort to maintain integration. Indeed, clearance of the Bottom put "extraordinary pressure" on Powelton, reopening "the threat of overcrowding and rent-gouging which had finally come under control in areas like Powelton Village."[55] The university's decision to buy $56,000 worth of shares in the PVDA to assist in the preservation of housing quite likely had a dampening effect on opposition. Similar support for other middle-class community organizations, which the university also invited to join the board of the West Philadelphia Corporation, helped further mute opposition.[56]

In the Bottom, however, residents organized with the help of Robert Coleman, an African American community organizer hired by Tabernacle Presbyterian Church, one of the few West Philadelphia Presbyterian churches that did not sell its building to an African American congregation and follow its parishioners to the suburbs. Located adjacent to Penn's campus where it used its student congregants as tutors in the community, Tabernacle was In-Ho Oh's church, and it felt a special obligation both to Oh and to the community in which he was killed. In support of its decision to stay in the neighborhood, the church had sponsored dances, helped youths find jobs, and supported group work with the Bottom youth gangs. The projects were not particularly successful, as work with gangs was suspended when their attendance at church-sponsored dances sparked conflict and efforts to find employment for local youths foundered on their lack of skills and education. Once Penn's plans for the Bottom became public, the church through Coleman organized demonstrations, community meetings, at which public officials acknowledged they had no plan for displaced residents, and eventually a sit-in at City Hall to protest the planned clearance of the area. The city agreed to recognize the community association as an unpaid consultant in forming the plans for the renewal area, but the group fractured over whether the focus should be on preserving existing housing or building new housing for residents on the vacated property. In the end, the WPC preserved a single street of houses, with a community organization as sponsor for their rehabilitation, and supported building a block of low-income housing nearby.[57]

Penn students became involved in protests, only over time, once it was revealed that the university and the Science Center had secret contracts with the Department of Defense for research on chemical and biological weapons. The students linked the war against Third World peoples in Southeast Asia to the war against colonized peoples in inner-city Philadelphia and won some significant concessions from the administration when it canceled the defense department contracts and agreed not to participate in any classified research in the future. But student involvement came too late for the Bottom.[58]

Despite opposition from community groups and students, Penn succeeded in clearing the Bottom because of the university's economic importance to the city of Philadelphia and its close ties to city redevelopment authorities, and because its proposal for University City fit well with the technocratic and planning-oriented approach to urban problems promoted by municipal and elected officials such as Richardson Dilworth. Philadelphia's postwar power elite argued that the city needed investment in its aging infrastructure, in its housing, and in its often cramped and small industrial plants. Civic groups, business associations, and the city's powerful universities supported the idea of an active government that used its resources as well as those garnered from the federal government in partnership with private enterprise to reengineer the spatial, economic, and social organization of the city.[59] Moreover, city authorities worried that Penn might decide to pull up stakes entirely and move its campus and its jobs to Valley Forge in the Philadelphia suburbs. Discussions within the Board of Trustees indicate that this was no idle threat, and the prospect was relinquished only when it became clear that the university's land needs in West Philadelphia would be met. Finally, the university's proximity to Center

City made the redevelopment of the campus area a logical extension of what already had been done downtown. Edmund Bacon, the doyen of city planners and executive director of the City Planning Commission, had moved buildings, streets, neighborhoods, and populations around as he remade the downtown neighborhood of Society Hill, the Center City retail district along Market Street, a new office complex near City Hall, and the city's transportation system. With plans for Center City well under way, West Philadelphia was an obvious next target. Although Bacon favored spot clearance and rehabilitation of historically significant housing, as had occurred in Society Hill, he was less influential than William Rafsky, the city's director of development and a member of Mayor Dilworth's cabinet—which Bacon was not—who favored taking a bulldozer to the city's slums. With Rafsky's support, Penn was authorized to proceed with clearing the Bottom. The University of Pennsylvania, with a physical plant estimated at $100 million in 1956, was determined to remake its environs rather than allowing its environs to remake it.[60]

The university's accomplishments in the Bottom, however, were far more modest than university and city officials had hoped. The Penn-dominated West Philadelphia Corporation demanded the complete demolition of buildings in the Bottom, which was its largest victory. About 20 percent of the vacant land was covered by the University City Science Center, which generated some science and medical research facilities but never to the degree its supporters predicted.[61] University City High School, intended to be a post-*Sputnik* elite science and technology school that would prepare students for the new world of scientific and medical research, was slated to occupy sixteen acres in the Bottom, or another 15 percent of the space. Local residents, who feared it would be a specialized school for the children of Penn and Drexel professors, demanded a regular city high school instead. When the high school opened, it had a larger catchment area than the West Philadelphia Corporation wanted, had no specialized entrance requirements, and never became the elite school they had originally conceived.[62] Plans for high-rise apartment buildings and residences for faculty and students in the clearance area never materialized. A few modest office buildings and International House, a modernist high-rise, occupied several blocks north of campus. Much of the former Bottom, some fifty years later, remained devoted to parking.

As for In-Ho Oh's accused killers, Penn hired the prominent attorney Charles Biddle to follow the cases, and here too the accomplishments were fewer than university administrators had hoped for. At the outset of the trials, Biddle met with District Attorney Victor Blanc and with his assistant, Thomas Reed, the African American assistant district attorney chosen to try the defendants, to discuss legal strategy. Biddle dropped in on Alfonso Borum's trial and met with Reed on several subsequent occasions. Reed faced off with Cecil B. Moore, the prominent civil rights leader and president of the Philadelphia chapter of the NAACP, who had volunteered to defend Borum. Reed won a rare death-penalty conviction against Borum, who as the oldest member and the alleged ringleader of the group and who had In-Ho Oh's blood splattered on his clothing, was tried first when anger was hottest. Following the conviction, Biddle wrote Gaylord Harnwell: "This is quite an accomplishment, for it is a long time since a Philadelphia jury has found a first degree verdict with the death penalty." Biddle worried, however, that mercy might be extended to Borum, adding, "I trust that the force of public opinion will be sufficient to prevent any misguided do-gooders in high places from commuting the sentence."[63]

Biddle was right to be concerned, as Borum's conviction was overturned on appeal. The appellate court held that it was prejudicial for Reed to introduce Borum's lengthy juvenile record into evidence and ordered the case retried. Borum was convicted a second time, but of second-degree murder, which did not carry the death penalty, and he was sentenced to a ten- to twenty-year term. (Borum was paroled in 1974, after serving sixteen years, and in 1979 returned to prison after being convicted of robbery, assault, and conspiracy.) Franklin Marshall was convicted of second-degree murder and sentenced to a ten- to twenty-year term as well. Douglas Clark and Leonard Johnson, each fifteen years old at the time of the crime, were convicted of first-degree murder and sentenced to life imprisonment, while three others, Harold Johnson, Robert Williams, and Percy Johnson, all served about five years for second-degree murder and were released in 1963. The McCloud brothers and James Wright, who had turned state's evidence, were each sentenced to ten years' probation. Lonnie Collins was the only defendant acquitted, after District Attorney Reed found the evidence against him unconvincing and asked for a directed not-guilty verdict.[64]

The most humane response to In-Ho Oh's murder came from his family. In a widely publicized letter to Harnwell, Oh's parents asked that "the most generous treatment possible within the laws of your government" be given to the youths who killed their son. "It is our hope that we may somehow be instrumental in the salvation of the souls, and in giving life to the human nature of the murderers." Twenty family members signed the letter and agreed to contribute to a fund for the "religious, educational, vocational, and social guidance of the boys when they are released." They asked that Oh be buried in Philadelphia "for your land too, is homeland for Christians and people of the democratic society."[65] Unfortunately, the amount of money the Oh family was able to raise—five hundred dollars—was too small to do much with. Eventually the money and the accumulated interest were returned to In-Ho Oh's uncle, for a club he ran for Korean students in West Philadelphia.[66]

In-Ho Oh's murder in 1958 reveals the social tensions inherent in the competition for space among racial groups in the postwar city, the inadequacy of government institutions and leaders in mediating that competition, and the use of urban renewal as a response to murder. While Penn succeeded in pushing back the boundaries of poor communities, in creating a science center, in supporting the development of a buffer zone of middle-class residences, and in unifying and beautifying its campus, it failed to accomplish the larger social goals implicit in the concept of a "university city." Three murders of Penn students between 1966 and 1970 and eight rapes on campus during the academic year of 1971–72 sparked widespread outrage and demands for better security both in campus buildings and in adjacent streets.[67] In the early 1990s, the murders of three Penn affiliates led to new, though more modest efforts, at urban renewal and redevelopment. Throughout the past fifty years, security has remained an elusive goal, even as the university has launched successive renewal plans.

Richardson Dilworth's noteworthy failure to inspire a progressive conversation about race, inequality, and murder in Philadelphia was indicative of a larger failure to confront both crime and the social conditions that spawned it. Most of his audience was unwilling, perhaps unable, to hear his message of both social and individual responsibility for crime, and Dilworth himself did not link the modernizing spatial and social policies he championed to worsening racial relations in the city. But the failure to

create a progressive dialogue about crime had broader and more dire consequences. White (and eventually African American) residents of the city
responded to the climate of fear created by violent crime by abandoning
older neighborhoods and sometimes supporting ever-more-repressive policies; institutions used urban renewal funds to reshape the city's geography
but rarely succeeded in keeping violence at bay; and conservative politicians
linked race and crime to their electoral advantage both locally and nationally. In these ways and others, murder proved to be central to the creation
of the urban crisis, to the history of the postwar city, and to the inability to
confront the implications of the growing carceral state.

## Chapter 4

# Dirty Work

## Police and Community Relations and the Limits of Liberalism

Decades of frustration about brutal treatment and police harassment exploded along North Philadelphia's Columbia Avenue on August 28, 1964. Like nearly all of the ghetto uprisings of the 1960s, this one began with a routine police action. Odessa Bradford quarreled with her husband, Rush, after their car stalled in the middle of a busy intersection. Rush stood outside the car yelling at his wife, while Odessa attempted to restart the engine. Both were drunk and the car wouldn't move. A police car arrived at the scene, and officers Robert Wells, an African American, and John Hoff, who was white, attempted to get Odessa to move the car. When she was unable to do so, the officers tried to extract her from behind the wheel. Friday-night revelers packed the bars near the intersection, and patrons gathered to watch the show outside. That one officer was black was less important than the fact that two police officers appeared to be mishandling a woman. The crowd grew increasingly restive as the officers wrestled with Odessa, and a bystander, James Mettles, struck Officer Hoff. His partner radioed an "assist officer" call, and a few minutes later a police wagon arrived along with other police cars. After placing everyone under arrest, the police cleared the intersection as bricks and bottles rained down from the roofs of nearby buildings. The presence of some twenty-five officers seemed to quell the disturbance, and police left.[1]

However, a rumor started in the neighborhood that a white police officer had either shot and killed a pregnant black woman or had beaten her to death in a jail cell. Such rumors of police killings inevitably swirled through black communities and sometimes directly precipitated a violent response.[2] Such stories seemed credible since abuse of black civilians by police was so common—physical violence to be sure, but also less extreme cases of discourtesy, the use of racist language, and harassment. Philadelphia police were notorious for using the "third degree" and severely beating suspects, as one black attorney put it, "before even asking the Negro if he committed the crime."[3] Feelings that police treated blacks unfairly, that they offered "neither justice nor protection," were widespread and of long standing, according to a study published by Philadelphia's Bureau of Municipal Research in 1947. The city police force was also a bastion of whiteness: in 1950, only 195 of 4,500 officers in the Philadelphia Police Department were black, a smaller percentage than had existed in the 1920s. Racism was entrenched in a department where a survey revealed that 59 percent of white officers objected to partnering with a black officer. In this environment, police mistreatment of black civilians was ignored, leading to bitter confrontations between police and community members. Incidents, such as police shootings, led to marches around City Hall in 1960 and a near riot in 1963. The 1964 uprising tapped a deep vein of existing grievances against police.[4]

The anger against police mistreatment boiled over as the rumor of Odessa Bradford's death spread. Crowds filled Columbia Avenue, a main street in North Philadelphia, which was already thick with pedestrians on a warm August night. A woman yelled to the crowd, "We're going to get an eye for an eye, a life for a life," while someone else hollered, "Let's run them out of North Philadelphia. Those white cops have no business up here." Shortly afterward, a police car heading up Columbia had its rear window broken by debris hurled by pedestrians, and an "assist officer" call drew police cars back to the area. Crowds attacked police, smashed store windows, and looted businesses along the main commercial streets, and police were unable to control them. Some six hundred police officers cordoned off the area to keep unrest from spreading farther.[5]

The uprising also made apparent the frustration of common folk with middle-class African American leaders and their liberal civil rights agenda. In the midst of the looting, African American ministers, political leaders, and civil rights activists rode through the streets on flatbed trucks and used megaphones to urge people to disperse. The largely young and male crowd (categorized as "hoodlums" by the mainstream black press) would have none of it and mocked middle-class black leaders. Judge Raymond Pace Alexander, the city's most prominent African American, told the crowd that looting only made things worse. Someone yelled in response, "Go home, you Uncle Tom. We don't need any handkerchief-head judges around here." Cecil B. Moore, the activist president of the National Association for the Advancement of Colored People (NAACP), who lived in the neighborhood and made his living as a firebrand criminal defense attorney, famously called more moderate civil rights leaders "part-time Negroes." Yet even Moore found himself stoned and jeered by the crowd—a measure of people's impatience with moderation. "We don't need civil rights," one yelled. "We can take care of ourselves."[6]

Police arrested rioters—308 altogether—but it was just a fraction of the total, and officers refrained from firing weapons or using other forms of force to suppress the disturbance. This became a major issue later as police claimed they had been "handcuffed" by their superiors. Police Commissioner Howard Leary had ordered police to keep their weapons holstered unless attacked and to leave their department-issued blackjacks in their back pockets unless absolutely necessary. Leary wanted to deescalate the situation and was willing to sacrifice property in return for fewer casualties, even though this alienated rank-and-file police officers.[7]

Leary's approach to the violence was controversial. Some African American leaders called for a sterner response, perhaps realizing that a community with few jobs and resources was in the process of losing even those. Obviously white business owners were angry at the loss of their properties and disagreed with Leary's handling of the violence. Observers noted Deputy Police Commissioner Frank Rizzo, popular with the rank and file, arguing heatedly with Leary about his orders. Afterward, however, the media and many public officials credited Leary for the restraint shown by Philadelphia police. Philadelphia suffered far fewer casualties than other American cities during the 1960s uprisings: only 2 people died and 339 were injured, including about 100 police officers. Leary's handling of the disturbance led directly to his appointment as police commissioner in New York City, which opened the door to Frank Rizzo's eventual appointment as a very different kind of police commissioner, one who emboldened Philadelphia police to act more aggressively.[8]

Investigations of 1960s urban uprisings pointed directly to police actions as immediate triggers to civil disturbances, and reform of police practices was one of the core demands of civil rights activists. Harlan Hahn, Judson Jeffries, Robert Fogelson, and Thomas Sugrue have all noted the relationship between police actions and civil disorders, while case studies by Leonard Moore on New Orleans, Matthew Countryman on Philadelphia, Dwight Watson on Houston, Patrick Jones on Milwaukee, and Tera Agyepong on Chicago explore more specific contexts of the police mistreatment of civilians that frequently worsened during the civil rights era as white supremacy was challenged.[9] While many other issues contributed to the civil unrest of the 1960s, the actions of police were the most readily visible. Unlike housing discrimination, overcrowded and segregated schools, limited employment opportunities, and general poverty, the perpetrators of police abuse were obvious and at hand. At the same time, police misbehavior seemed more remediable, if only because it did not require vast changes in public attitude or large infusions of federal money. A coalition of interracial liberals—the American Civil Liberties Union (ACLU), the NAACP, the Congress of Racial Equality (CORE), and other civil rights activists— promoted civilian review of police actions as the best check on abusive policing. As Martha Biondi has noted, demands for civilian review became a staple of civil rights activism as early as the 1940s, and a generation later, the Kerner Commission recommended civilian review as a necessary reform in its report on civil disorders.[10]

Yet Philadelphia already had a civilian review board, the first such independent board in the nation, established in 1958. Despite that, the city had exploded with the same rage found in other cities. Indeed, that uprising contributed to the eventual demise of Philadelphia's Police Advisory Board (PAB) and to New York City's fractious debate over civilian review. Historians have analyzed the defeat of a civilian review board in New York City, but little attention has been paid to the PAB, the nation's first and longest-lived board.[11] And although there is a growing literature on police and police-community relations, many historians, as Themis Chronopoulos has noted, "have taken the antagonistic police-community relationship for granted."[12] The case files of the PAB, although incomplete, provide evidence of the fractious relations between police and members of minority communities in the period leading up to and immediately following the 1964 civil

disturbance.[13] The turbulent history of the PAB, which was eliminated by
Mayor James Tate in 1969 at the behest of then police commissioner Frank
Rizzo, thus provides an ideal lens through which to view the limitations of
postwar liberalism, the difficulties of police reform, and the endemic nature
of police-minority community violence.

Police-minority community violence was endemic because police were
"dirty workers," in sociologist Lee Rainwater's phrase, performing tasks
that mainstream society wanted done but did not wish to recognize
overtly.[14] The dirty workers' role was to confine and control outgroups,
submerged and disenfranchised people, and for police in the United States
this has frequently meant African Americans. Increasingly in the twentieth
century, as black urban populations swelled from migration, dirty work
meant upholding the informal apartheid found in American cities. Intensive policing—car stops, frisks, and frequent searches of persons and
property—concentrated in minority communities in part because of their
high crime rates but also as a way of controlling and surveilling a restive
population.[15] As dirty work, however, the police's maintenance of racial
order could not be directly acknowledged—in fact it was officially denied—
and therefore it was not something learned in training manuals or found
in directives from police headquarters. Rather, new officers learned how to
patrol minority communities as part of the informal norms of policing, the
"street knowledge" or "worklore" imparted by veterans.[16] Moreover, with
mid-twentieth-century police forces still dominated by white ethnic, frequently Irish Catholic, males, intensive policing of black neighborhoods
could take the form of self-interest with the intent of containing a population threatening established white ethnic neighborhoods.[17] Official tolerance for different standards of policing for different communities and for
all but the most extreme examples of police abuse helped convert individual
self-interest into collective dirty work. Since civilian review threatened to
subject such actions to public scrutiny, police and their supporters vehe-
mently resisted it in Philadelphia and prevented its implementation in
other cities, such as New York, when it was proposed. Opponents argued
that civilians could never judge police actions fairly, that civilian review was
subversive of public order, and that any complaint about an officer could
only be handled internally by the police department. What white liberals

and civil rights advocates wanted to expose, police and their supporters wished to leave covered up. Dirty work by its very nature had to remain under wraps.

The creation of Philadelphia's review board was the last product of the interracial liberals' agenda to shape the city in the 1950s. A coalition of "young Turks," supported by black and ethnic white voters, Americans for Democratic Action, and business interests tired of the corruption of Philadelphia's Republican machine and concerned about the visible decay of the city, marched into power in 1951 with the election of Joseph Clark as mayor and Richardson Dilworth as district attorney. Simultaneously, a new home rule charter banned discrimination in public employment, housing, and accommodations and established a Commission on Human Relations to investigate discriminatory practices. The reformers wanted to open Philadelphia government up to those previously unrepresented, including African Americans, but they were primarily interested in good government. They wanted to make meritorious rather than patronage appointments and to bring expertise to bear on the city's social and economic problems, so theirs was a technocratic liberalism as much as one concerned with civil rights and social justice.[18] As district attorney, Dilworth responded to demands from the civil rights community for inclusion by appointing the first African Americans and women to the DA's office in the city's history, thus brightening the prospects for interracial liberalism. But by the time Dilworth succeeded Clark as mayor in 1956, the interracial coalition that had supported reform was showing signs of fracture. Urban renewal of the city's downtown, which appealed to the city's business elite, had worsened a crisis of affordable housing; white homeowners, who had supported the idea of more responsive government, opposed the movement of African Americans into their neighborhoods; and Dilworth's proposal for scattered-site public housing was blocked in city council.[19] Although Democrats had cemented their control over the city's power structure, passage of civil rights–related legislation had become more difficult as reform Democrats were outmaneuvered by "regulars" more attentive to white ethnic voters than to African Americans. When concerns about police practices grew too numerous to ignore by the late 1950s, the city council held hearings but was unable to agree on a legislative remedy.

Civilian review of police actions had not been part of the original set of reform proposals enacted in the early 1950s as attention focused more on an unfolding police corruption scandal and removing the Republican machine's holdover appointments to the police department. As a result, the city charter left the police commissioner, who received the recommendations of a Police Trial Board, with the sole authority to discipline police officers. The Trial Board, which consisted of three members of the police department, focused on internal disciplinary issues brought by superior officers, not civilian complaints, and the Philadelphia ACLU found that not a single civilian complaint about police abuse had been upheld by the department's internal review process. Anger at police raids of numbers-writing establishments (illegal lotteries) that often were in people's homes or in storefront businesses led to city council hearings on police practices in 1957. Concerns about warrantless searches soon expanded to include other forms of abuse of city residents, particularly African Americans. Henry Sawyer, the president of the Philadelphia ACLU who was also a city council member and a key ally of Mayor Dilworth, introduced a bill to establish a civilian review board. When the council rejected it, Sawyer convinced Mayor Dilworth to bypass the legislative body by using his executive authority to establish it in the fall of 1958.[20]

The Police Review Board, as it was initially titled, was charged with investigating complaints brought to it by any party (not necessarily the victim) concerning police abuse, racial or religious discrimination, or a violation of state or constitutional rights. Any member of the five-person board, all of whom were appointed by the mayor, could order an investigation, but before any punitive action could be recommended to the police commissioner, a police officer had the right to a public hearing and legal representation. At least three members had to be present for the hearing, and a majority had to agree on a recommendation.[21]

The review board faced immediate challenges. Since Dilworth established it by executive order, the board confronted significant financial and administrative hurdles. Miffed at the mayor, the city council refused to appropriate money for support of the board, and the five-member volunteer body had neither subpoena power nor an investigative staff. Although the city council eventually appropriated sufficient funding to hire a part-time executive director and a secretary, the other administrative problems were never addressed, and the board never received any independent legislative authorization, meaning that any future mayor could eliminate it. Its

investigations continued to be conducted by members of the police department, and any disciplinary sanctions it proposed were only recommendations to the police commissioner, who had the sole power to implement
them.[22]

Despite the obvious weaknesses of the review board, it faced immediate
political opposition from the Fraternal Order of Police (FOP), which represented the interests of police rank and file. The FOP, which had argued that
there would be a "revolt" in the department if the board were created, filed
a court challenge requesting an injunction against the board's operations,
alleging that its creation exceeded the mayor's authority. The FOP and the
city avoided legal confrontation by reaching a face-saving agreement that
renamed the board the Police Advisory Board (the city charter stated that
the mayor had the power to appoint advisory boards, although that did
not prevent two later court challenges from the FOP on similar grounds).
According to the agreement, investigations could be requested but not
ordered, an investigation of a police officer's conduct would be postponed
until any criminal charges against him were resolved, and the FOP retained
the right to represent officers at a hearing, while the board remained largely
toothless administratively.[23]

The national office of the FOP, located in Philadelphia, continued to
fulminate about the PAB and proposals to create civilian review boards in
other cities. The FOP asked how police could do their jobs if they "are
bound in chains" and argued that the real purpose of review boards was to
undermine police forces and sap police morale. Asking who would benefit
from the collapse of law and order in the United States, the FOP answered,
"There is no question that the boards can serve as spearheads for the Com-
munists."[24] Despite the overblown rhetoric emanating from the national
office, the Philadelphia FOP called a truce with the Police Advisory Board
after the 1960 settlement with the city, only resuming its guerrilla warfare
against the board following the civil disturbances in 1964.

The most obvious reason for the Philadelphia FOP's quiescence, even
as the national office continued to agitate, lay in the structure and function-
ing of the board. The compromise with the city established an official role
for the FOP in hearings, and since the FOP would only represent members,
it incentivized police officers to join in case charges were ever filed against
them.[25] The national FOP's extreme rhetoric also helped in a backhanded

way. By raising the specter of hostile panels predisposed to second-guess an officer's actions, it highlighted the local FOP's role as sole defender of the ordinary police officer.

The advisory board also acted very cautiously in this politically fraught atmosphere. The cumulative effect of the FOP lawsuit, the reliance on volunteers to staff hearing panels, the use of police department investigators, the lack of enthusiasm for the board by factions within the Democratic Party, and a general absence of publicity meant the PAB investigated only 32 complaints in its first year. Thereafter, activity picked up with 75 complaints in its second year and 107 in its third.[26] The vast majority of these complaints were settled informally in a meeting with the executive director, where, according to the board, most complainants left satisfied once their concerns had been aired. Other complaints were settled with an apology from the police officer or with an agreement to expunge the record of an unjustified arrest, but in cases where a police action was legitimate, with an explanation of the law to a complainant. The board may have exaggerated its salutary effects on Philadelphia's citizenry when it argued that it was a safety valve in police-community relations, but at the conclusion of its fourth year, only 12 complaints advanced as far as a public hearing out of 108 cases closed. Only 6 of those 12 cases were decided against the police, again suggesting the caution with which the board operated.[27] It is therefore not surprising that Police Commissioner Thomas Gibbons, who initially opposed civilian review, when asked whether or not the board had lowered the morale of the police, stated, "Well, if you talk to some individual officer who has appeared before the Board, then I guess the answer would be that this has a harmful effect, but from my point of view as Commissioner, I think the Board has not only aided me, but has aided the Police Department."[28] The simple existence of an independent review board seemed to some to make a difference. Philadelphia's Urban League head Andrew Freeman claimed in 1964 that since the PAB's creation, there had been a steady decline in the number of brutality charges lodged against police.[29]

The case records of the PAB provide the basis for a less sanguine conclusion. Even if the vast majority of complaints were settled informally or with the complainant failing to follow up, patterns of police harassment are clearly visible in the records. Police targeted interracial groups for particular attention and initiated questioning in the absence of any complaint or evidence of wrongdoing. This served as a form of boundary maintenance as people who were "out of place" were de facto targets of suspicion. Spencer Coxe, the executive director of the ACLU and one of the five members of the PAB board, commented that even orderly social gatherings taking place in private residences were raided, "apparently solely on the grounds that both whites and Negroes were present." As a result of these incidents, the mayor warned the police department that the interracial nature of a gathering was not grounds for intervention.[30] Nonetheless harassment continued. An interracial group returning from an amusement park, where scuffles had broken out with white park visitors, found themselves harassed and one of their number arrested when police stormed onto their train on returning to the city. The board repeatedly requested an end to police stops and interrogations that seemed based only on the interracial background of a group.[31] A few years later, Mercer Tate, an attorney and former chairman of the PAB, supplied an affidavit based on his experience in support of a lawsuit against the Philadelphia Police Department, alleging discriminatory treatment of African Americans. Tate cited "the stopping of interracial couples for no reason other than . . . the mixing of races" as an ongoing practice.[32] A white minister driving with a young black woman complained that they were stopped on the grounds of suspected prostitution, something police frequently cited as the reason for questioning interracial couples. The board again requested that the police commissioner issue a directive forbidding police from investigating mixed groups without evidence of a crime.[33] While this might suggest that the board acted effectively, the fact that complaints continued over the lifetime of the PAB indicate that it was better at revealing the contours of dirty work than in preventing it.

Commanding public space and controlling those who moved through it were fundamental parts of a police officer's job regardless of where he was stationed, but in black neighborhoods it took on the added significance of reinforcing racial hierarchy. In the city's working-class row-house neighborhoods, where lounging on street corners or sitting on stoops was a common leisure time activity, especially in the heat of the summer, police would tell groups to move on and inquire where they lived. Needless to say, the experiences of being stopped and questioned, of being frisked and prodded, of feeling under surveillance even on one's own block or doorstep, provoked deep resentment of police and seemed particularly oppressive. One woman, a community activist involved with the public schools, wrote, "In my experience, the police consider black people to be less than human and subject them to special oppressive tactics. These tactics involve daily frisking, questioning and detaining. My children grew up realizing that a part of life was to be constantly stopped by the police without any reason given." She noted that police behavior had changed over time. When she first moved to the neighborhood, it was white, and "the police were nice and respectful. . . . But when the color of the area changed, so did the police service. Things have become terrible and the police are always on our backs."[34]

Car stops compounded the frustration with police. One man, writing in September 1962, said he was stopped and taken to the police station, where he and his car were searched. The search did not yield anything incriminatory, and he was released; but he complained that this was the seventh time he had been stopped since June. As Jonathan Rubinstein noted in his 1960s ethnographic study of Philadelphia police officers, the police felt they had an "unqualified right" under Pennsylvania law to stop any car on a public street and check the license and registration, and they frequently did so. Usually stops occurred for some minor traffic violation, such as not signaling for a turn or failing to come to a complete stop at a stop sign, or from equipment failure, such as a broken tail light. Car stops and writing tickets generated activity for a police officer, which increased the opportunity for getting noticed by the brass and earning a promotion and perhaps for making a good arrest if a driver or passenger had an outstanding warrant. Such stops concentrated in "high crime," usually black, neighborhoods and did not add appreciably to public safety, though they certainly added to the black public's irritation. In cases where a stop and search revealed nothing illegal, drivers felt violated—targeted for racial reasons—and their frustration could boil over into confrontation, especially if police became abusive as their authority was questioned.[35]

The disrespectful language used by police in such confrontations accounted for about one-third of all complaints.[36] One man was ordered out of his car with "hey, boy, get out of that car." When he objected that he was twenty-five and no longer a boy, the officer allegedly said, "You're not only a boy, but a damn Nigger." This sort of thing happened sufficiently frequently that the Reverend (later Representative) William Gray III, when he served as chairman of the PAB, wrote to Mayor James Tate asking for a mayoral directive to the police: "It was emphatically stated by Mr. B . . . that the officer referred to him repeatedly as 'boy.' While Officer M . . . denied this, it is the Board's feeling that the use of this salutation by Officer M . . . had much to do with the personality clashes which ensued and culminated in Mr. B's arrest. The Board has received repeated complaints from Negro citizens that they have been addressed as 'boy' by officers. We would like to respectfully suggest that you caution the police against such salutation because of historical sensitivity of minority groups to such terms."[37]

Searches of homes, with or without warrants, were a persistent problem, especially when residents in poor communities relied on the informal economy to make a living. While the informal economy operated in white, low-income communities as well, the intensive policing of black communities made these activities more visible to authorities. Moreover, there were numerous complaints that police arrested low-level operators while ignoring the white organized-crime members who frequently oversaw illegal enterprise. Writing numbers, selling alcohol after hours, dealing narcotics, making moonshine, and hosting card games in return for a percentage of the pot generated income for people who had little opportunity for legal employment. Raids without actual search warrants raised the issue of corruption, as cash was frequently seized, and those arrested were simply held overnight and never formally charged. One shoeshine shop owner complained that on two different occasions police raided his quarters, which also served as his home, no doubt suspecting gambling, without a warrant and harassed his customers. Both times he was arrested for running a disorderly house, but the charges were dropped. Another woman complained indignantly that while she played the numbers, she did not write them, and despite being found with slips of paper, the trial magistrate dismissed the charges against her. Similarly, the owner of a beauty shop complained that police raided her business with a warrant alleging that it was a numbers collection site, but nothing was found and no charges were filed.[38] Arrests of small-time black hustlers, while police meanwhile allegedly took bribes to ignore major gamblers or drug dealers, fueled the sense of injustice that police padded their arrest records with people struggling to get by.[39]

Officers serving arrest or "body" warrants crashed through the doors of people's homes, and taking control of the space often involved physically subduing residents.[40] One officer serving a notice for a suspect to appear at police district headquarters encountered resistance from the suspect's mother and fourteen-year-old brother. According to one PAB account, "As he handed the message to Mrs. B . . . a young boy [who was on crutches for a broken leg] came to the door and began to berate him using profanity. He told the boy to keep quiet but he continued to abuse the officer. In the meantime, a large crowd was congregating around the porch and steps." As the officer attempted to arrest the boy for breach of peace, he apparently knocked him over. Finding his entry into the house then blocked by the mother, the officer returned to his car to call for assistance. He and fellow officers then charged into the house and "began to beat Ronald with their clubs causing him to fall to the floor. Someone kicked him in the groin. Officer S . . . was on top of Ronald and began to choke him . . . and Ronald finally passed out." Several officers testified that the boy had used one of his crutches to swing at the officers and that they had simply used force to subdue him and effect his arrest. In this case, the PAB decided that the incident had been initiated by the family's resistance to receiving a summons, that injuries in the melee were insignificant and did not appear to sustain the family's account, concluding that no disciplinary action was necessary.[41]

Brutality charges accounted for nearly half (43 percent) of all complaints to the board. About two-thirds of all complaints to the board were made by blacks in a city in which they composed only about a quarter of the population. But when it came to the use of force, Philadelphia police brutalized both whites and blacks, at least as suggested by the filing of complaints—whites submitted 30 percent of brutality complaints versus 32 percent by blacks—and the training officers emphasized taking quick and often physical command of a situation regardless of the race of an arrestee. Nonetheless, the fact that a disproportionate number of all complainants were black reflected the nature of the dirty work involved in policing minority communities.[42]

If an officer's mere presence was insufficient to command obedience, a physical confrontation frequently followed. The case records make clear that police demanded immediate obedience to their directives, and even asking an officer the reason for a car or pedestrian stop was sometimes enough to set off an altercation. The tools of the trade were designed to inflict sufficient pain so as to make a prolonged fight unlikely. A police officer used a nightstick to jab the midsection or the ribs, or to rake across the shins and other bones, to break a nose, hand, or an ankle if necessary. Officers might bring out a blackjack from a back pocket for use close to the body in order to concuss a suspect with a quick, sharp blow to the head. Despite the hierarchical command structure and military organization of police forces, a lot had to be left to an officer's discretion since commanders had little opportunity for direct supervision. Commanders had to trust their officers, and there was minimum second-guessing. An attack on a police officer was an attack on public order and ultimately on the state's authority, and officers knew that they could subdue a suspect by any means necessary. If a suspect complained, officers would be supported by their commanders, by the district attorney, and usually by the courts.[43]

Suspects maintained that police beat them as part of an "alley court" arrest, especially if charges were flimsy and the police thought that the suspect might beat the rap. The worse the beating, generally the more serious and more numerous the charges levied against a suspect. As the PAB noted, "It seemed to be standard police procedure to charge a person with resisting arrest or disorderly conduct wherever the person charges the police with brutality." These charges, known as "cover charges," gave the district attorney leeway for a plea bargain or for negotiating the dropping of charges in return for a complainant not seeking legal redress against an arresting officer.[44] Jonathan Rubinstein recounted the capture of a child molester who was held in custody at the station house: "Any squad member who wished was allowed to beat the suspect from the ankles to the armpits with his stick. Men came off the street to participate in the beating and then returned to patrol." The criminal justice system was slow, and police in exercising curbstone justice saw themselves as quick and effective enforcers of moral as well as racial order.[45]

The PAB was as reluctant as other arms of the criminal justice system to second-guess police in the use of force. In one instance, where a mother lodged a complaint that her son had been arrested for throwing rocks and was then beaten with a nightstick and required hospital treatment, the board concluded there was "insufficient evidence" of wrongdoing. "There is an obvious conflict in the testimony between M . . . , who was supported and corroborated by his mother, and Q . . . , who was supported and corroborated by his fellow officers." The charges against the officer were not supported by the independent evidence "necessary to take action which might adversely affect a police officer's entire career." Police covered for one another, and in view of conflicting testimony and the murky line between necessary and excessive force, the PAB gave the police the benefit of the doubt.[46]

The PAB's record of hearing citizens' complaints and reprimanding officers for abuses of power was disappointing at best. Fairly or not, community critics came to perceive the PAB as being pro-police because of the small number of complaints that it found justified.[47] Out of 932 cases brought in its nine years of operation, the PAB recommended that 20 officers be suspended, 30 reprimanded, and one fired.[48] Despite this seemingly anemic record, civil rights liberals, like the Urban League's Andrew Freeman, lauded the PAB, which was also defended by coalitions of African American ministers, the Fellowship Commission, and the *Philadelphia Tribune*, the city's African American newspaper.[49] The board retained support from moderates, who saw no contradiction between civil rights and law and order, but who wanted better police service and hoped the PAB might help deliver it.[50] Supporters acknowledged the PAB's limitations— most of which were structural ones, stemming from its origins in an executive order, or political ones, deriving from the board's awareness of its tenuous public support—but continued to see it as an answer to police abuse and a way of relieving community tension.

The view from the streets was different. The PAB had not been able to stop police abuses, few police officers had been punished, and activists began to discourage people from reporting incidents in what seemed like a futile enterprise. Increasingly, radical activists attacked both police and moderate civil rights leaders, and to the degree that their voices reflected a broader shift in black popular opinion, the work of institutions such as the PAB became untenable. Civilian review was a decidedly moderate response to police abuse, one that held that the problem was an individual one, fixable through reprimands and suspensions of officers that deterred other police from committing similar offenses, and preventable by adding community relations courses to police academy training. It did not confront the essential task of policing, the unacknowledged dirty work needed to control a subjugated population, which was systemic and institutional, not

individual.[51] The violence directed against police during the 1964 disturbance indicates that the PAB's role as a "safety valve" was exaggerated, an
optimistic fantasy promoted by the city's moderate civil rights leadership.
And as the PAB lost support on the left, it came under increasing attack
from the right.

The PAB's death throes began with the 1964 Columbia Avenue riot,
which initiated a rising crescendo of conservative critiques. Police argued
that they had been handcuffed by fear of brutality charges, a claim later
echoed by the Federal Bureau of Investigation's J. Edgar Hoover, who also
called review boards "sidewalk kangaroo courts."[52] John Harrington, who
twice ran unsuccessfully for election as president of the local FOP before
discovering the police advisory board issue, castigated the FOP's leadership
for its lack of aggressiveness in opposing the board. He blamed the board
for declining respect for law and order, declaring, "Minority groups don't
fear arrest. They spit and curse officers and refuse to obey laws because they
know policemen can't arrest them."[53] Harrington also used the PAB's caution against it, saying twenty-three reprimands and three temporary suspensions of police officers since 1958 proved that police were doing their
jobs and the board was not needed.[54] The city's mainstream newspapers in
their coverage of the riot stressed that the police had stood down, afraid to
intervene, which was now blamed on the PAB, providing further fodder for
its critics.[55] When discussing the Columbia Avenue disorder, Harrington
claimed erroneously that ten square miles of the city had been destroyed
by rioters, and he argued that "police . . . were trained in the use of night
sticks and blackjacks but were afraid to use them." Harrington claimed that
only after hearing from Mayor Tate that no one would be taken before the
PAB for manhandling a rioter, which he conveyed to the rank and file, was
the riot extinguished "in four hours." Harrington used his charges against
civilian review boards to vault into the leadership of both the local and the
national FOP and to convince white voters that police were not afraid to
do the dirty work necessary to maintain public order.[56]

That virtually all of this was fantasy did not matter. As Spencer Coxe of
the PAB pointed out in a letter to the *Philadelphia Inquirer*, the city's second
largest daily, ten square miles would have added up to 1,200 blocks, when
"actually, the stores that were severely damaged, along perhaps two miles
of streets could probably be fitted into a few city blocks." That Philadelphia

suffered few casualties and less damage than other cities did not seem to matter in countering conservative demagoguery.[57]

The FOP's battle against the advisory board was overshadowed by the tumultuous debate over the creation of a civilian review board in New York City, which drew national attention. Demagoguery reached its crescendo in New York City, where the John Birch Society worked with the Police Benevolent Association (New York's version of the FOP) to organize demonstrations outside City Hall against civilian review and in support of police. Two separate efforts to pass legislation in city council failed, but John Lindsay made civilian review of police part of his election campaign. When he took office as mayor in 1966, the campaign for civilian review resurged. Lindsay proposed adding four civilians to an existing three-person police department review board, a compromise position, and hired Philadelphia's Howard Leary to reform the New York City Police Department. The PBA, with the help of the Conservative Party and community groups, collected 100,000 signatures to force a referendum and then ran a grassroots campaign against civilian review funded by national conservative organizations. Despite support from New York's liberal icons—Republican senator Jacob Javits and Democratic senator Robert Kennedy headed a pro–review board coalition—the civilian review board was rejected by a crushing margin. In this bastion of liberalism, 63 percent out of a near record two million votes were cast against it.[58]

The PBA and conservative politicians played on fear of crime and disorder and used thinly veiled racial appeals to stir the electorate. Economic decline, structural shifts in the job market, the social dislocation caused by urban renewal projects, and racism all played a role in the way voters responded to the referendum. But so did New York City's rising crime rate: the annual number of murders increased steadily from 390 in 1960 to 631 in 1965, a 61 percent jump. Murder, like other crime, was spatialized and racialized, concentrating in specific police precincts that covered low-income black neighborhoods, but fear of crime was widespread. The percentage of murders in the nation's largest cities grew significantly in the same five-year period: in Los Angeles, 62 percent; Chicago, 8 percent, Philadelphia, 37 percent; and Detroit, 25 percent.[59] Such startling increases over a short period fed anxiety about crime more generally. In this context, one did not have to be a racist to fear a proposal that allegedly "handcuffed" police, and opponents of civilian review exploited that fear adroitly.

The FOP's Harrington, sensing an opportunity after the Columbia Avenue disturbance and the political turmoil around civilian review in New York, initiated a new court challenge to the advisory board in 1965. The FOP argued that the PAB's creation was not authorized by the city charter, a matter that had been left unsettled after the out-of-court compromise between the FOP and the city in 1960. The FOP now sought an injunction to keep the board from holding hearings, which was granted in September 1965. Meanwhile, following the departure of the executive director, Mayor Tate failed to make a new appointment for the first six months of 1965—reflecting his ambivalence about civilian review in the wake of the 1964 disturbance. And once a new director was appointed, the police department informed him that its officers were too busy handling civil rights demonstrations to be able to serve as investigators in abuse cases. Although the injunction against the PAB was lifted in the spring of 1966, nearly fifteen months of only limited activity took its toll. Complaints had accumulated with no professional staff to review them, no police to investigate them, and no hearing panels to decide them. Although the board resumed its work, the delays added to doubts within the city's already skeptical working-class black community about the PAB's effectiveness and willingness to confront police abuse. Then all the stonewalling paid off the following year, when Court of Common Pleas judge Leo Weinrott decided in favor of the Fraternal Order of Police and ordered the PAB disbanded in March 1967, declaring that Mayor Dilworth had in fact exceeded his authority in creating the board.[60]

Mayor James Tate, an Irish-Catholic machine Democrat who lacked the reforming zeal of the Clark-Dilworth liberal coalition, did not mourn the court's decision. While the PAB's supporters urged the mayor to appeal, Tate dawdled, reflecting his reading of the political winds. With a mayoral election on the horizon, doing nothing probably seemed like the best option. Tate did not want to jeopardize his standing with moderate black leaders by declaring the board dead or with the FOP and its white supporters by initiating an appeal. Only the threat by individual members of the board to hire their own lawyers to defend what was in fact a city agency finally forced Tate's hand.[61]

Tate had decided to marry his political fortunes to Frank Rizzo, appointing him as acting police commissioner shortly after the Democratic primary in 1967, knowing that it would cement his standing among crime-fearing white voters before the general election. Like most police officers, Rizzo was a constant critic of the PAB, and he took his cue from the FOP's Harrington, arguing that the board's inability to find patterns of abuse or even very many individual infractions proved that the board was unnecessary. As commissioner, Rizzo declared categorically, "Police abuse absolutely does not exist in Philadelphia." Pointing to only one instance where any police officers had been convicted in a court of law, he called evidence of police abuse a media fabrication.[62] Although the city's appeal of Judge Weinrott's decision to disband the PAB wended its way through the higher courts for two more years, the end of the board was in sight.

The PAB, however, refused to go quickly or quietly. The city finally "won" its court case in June 1969, when the Pennsylvania Supreme Court reversed the lower court. The PAB issued a press release that it was being reconstituted, but then nothing happened. Regardless of the court decision upholding the PAB's legitimacy, no one could force the mayor to make it operational. Tate signaled his intentions, declaring "Commissioner Rizzo does not want . . . [the PAB], and if Commissioner Rizzo does not want it, I do not want it."[63] Hoping that he could kill the board without fanfare, Tate left it in limbo, still in existence, but with the office furniture removed, the office space reassigned to another agency, and the secretary posted to another job, all without notification to the board. The chairman, Mercer Tate (no relation to the mayor), wrote the mayor a public letter saying, "Your actions now make it apparent that you have irrevocably decided to prohibit any independent review of police activities."[64]

If Chairman Tate was gambling that he could embarrass the mayor into reassembling the PAB, he was wrong. Since the PAB still existed, albeit as a shadow of its former self, Tate announced it would hold its first public hearing in two years. While there were any number of cases Tate might have picked, he chose to review the killing of Isaiah McFadden Davis, which had occurred on New Year's Day in 1966, nearly four years earlier. Davis's killing by an off-duty police officer was particularly egregious. No issue was more readily guaranteed to create controversy, which seemed to be Tate's intent. He declared, "I expect that after our first hearing that Rizzo will explode and that Mayor Tate might even dissolve the board," adding, "I have been expecting a phone call from him all week . . . telling me that he was doing that."[65]

In the absence of city office space, the hearing was scheduled for the White Hope Baptist Church, which made it seem more like a community meeting than an official hearing. Commissioner Rizzo ordered his police not to cooperate with the panel, but the board had several eyewitnesses willing to appear as well as a record of the medical examiner's inquest into Davis's death, at which the two officers involved in the shooting, John J. Boyd and John Thomas Jr., had testified. In an act of political theater, as witnesses appeared, Tate repeatedly asked if anyone was there from the police department who wished to cross-examine, but as he expected, "no one identified himself as a policeman."[66]

The medical examiner's record provided the most complete testimony about the shooting, at least from the police's perspective. Boyd and Thomas had been at a New Year's Eve party when someone told Boyd that his car had been stolen and was seen careening down the street. The officers, both in plainclothes, decided to drive around the neighborhood looking for the car, which they spotted parked on a nearby street, with the ignition torn out. Since the hood was still warm and an overcoat was in the back seat, they concluded that the car thieves would be nearby, and so they disabled the starter and decided to lie in wait for their return.

When nineteen-year-old Isaiah Davis and fifteen-year-old William Rainey got in the car and attempted to start it, Officer Thomas pulled his car up and blocked the passenger-side door, while Boyd jumped out and ran to the driver. Thomas said Boyd had his badge out and identified himself as a police officer, and he did the same. "By the time I got around the opposite side, Officer Boyd had the door open and was scuffling." Neither youth would get out of the car, and Thomas recalled, "Finally I started pulling him [Rainey] out of the car. He kept on swinging. After I got him outside the car, he was swinging and kicking; so, I had the revolver in my hand. I hit him on the head a couple times." After getting Rainey "quieted down," he turned and saw Davis backed up against a wall with a knife in his hand facing Boyd; Rainey took the opportunity to slip his grasp and run away, and while Thomas went in chase, he heard a shot fired, turned, and saw Davis lying on the pavement.

Officer Boyd amplified Thomas's account, saying the shooting was an accident. After repeatedly telling Davis that he was under arrest and that he should stop fighting, Boyd claimed that Davis pulled a knife and slashed at him. Boyd hit him several times with the revolver. "So, he jerked loose, and he grabbed this milk crate and came back with the milk crate and hit me. I leaned back and kicked. When I kicked, I fell back . . . [and] my arm hit the pole. That's all the pressure was needed to set it [the revolver] off because I had a tight grip on it."

Other officers, who arrived at the scene, recalled seeing Davis lying in a pool of blood; no one recalled seeing a knife at the scene, though one was produced later by the police, and William Rainey, the surviving youth, allegedly identified the knife to police as one taken from his mother's kitchen.

Rainey's version of the incident was different. He said, " 'We went to get out of the car but before we could one man grabbed Davis and the other grabbed me. They start beating up on our heads with pistols.' " Rainey eluded Thomas's grasp and ran up the street to his grandmother's house: "Thomas stopped chasing me and I heard a shot." He admitted that Davis had a screwdriver with him so he could pop the ignition on a car, but he denied that either of them had knives, and he stated that he had never seen the knife that police produced. Rainey's grandmother also stated emphatically, "I never saw that knife before." When confronted with his statement to police in which he identified the knife, Rainey said, "I told him I had a knife like it at home, but I didn't say it was the knife." An eyewitness, Lydia Coppedge, largely corroborated Rainey's testimony, though she was watching Thomas chase Rainey and did not see the actual shooting.[67]

Despite the medical examiner's conclusion that Davis died as a result of a homicide; that the concentration of blows on Davis's skull, which made him nearly unrecognizable, contradicted Boyd's account of a free-swinging melee; and that the force needed to pull the trigger on Boyd's service revolver was greater than an accidental jarring of his arm could cause, the grand jury declined to indict Boyd, and the case was closed.

The PAB had no legal standing to reopen a nearly four-year-old murder case. The board could only hear evidence, partial as it was, and hope to expose the abusive practices that were the essence of dirty work. Tate concluded the hearing by saying the board would review the testimony and the medical examiner's records and decide whether or not the case qualified as one of police abuse. But before any conclusions could be drawn, Mayor Tate dissolved the PAB.[68] Police Commissioner Rizzo called the decision a Christmas present to the police.

The PAB represented a quintessential expression of interracial liberalism and the faith that there were governmental solutions to difficult social problems. The liberal coalition of patrician reformers, business elites, working-class whites, and African Americans that had swept the corrupt Republican machine out of power combined disparate class and racial interests and was inherently unstable. By the late 1950s, even as the review board was being created, ties among the groups began to unravel. The board's structural weaknesses were a legacy of these divisions, leading the city council to reject civilian review and forcing the board to rely solely on the mayor's executive power. This hampered the board's operations from its start. The PAB lost support among African Americans for its tepid handling of police abuse accusations, and then, while the police did everything in their power to stymie the board, it succumbed to fears among whites that even a modest attempt to confront abuses by officers shackled the police and prevented them from defending public order. The 1964 disturbance on Columbia Avenue crystalized these conflicting views and signaled the failure of the PAB as a solution to community-police relations, even as civilian review was being proposed for other cities.

More importantly, civilian review could not solve the problem it was created to confront. Even with the more aggressive stance taken in its final year, the PAB never moved beyond its position that police abuse of minority citizens was the product of individual officers rather than evidence of institutional and systemic racism. The board retained a case-by-case approach, and it relied on both the goodwill of complainants to place their faith in a fact-finding, legalistic response to police abuse and the educability of individual police officers. Ultimately neither assumption proved correct. Many African Americans, as evidenced by the 1964 riot, had lost faith in liberal solutions to police abuse, while the police resisted any effort to subject their work to public scrutiny and rallied the white public behind them. The disbanding of the PAB meant civilian review of police was a dead issue in Philadelphia for another twenty-five years.[69]

While whites did suffer from police abuse—as the records of the PAB attest—it is also clear that much of the white public supported the police in enacting curbstone justice. There was no referendum per se on civilian review in Philadelphia, but Frank Rizzo, running for mayor as "America's toughest cop," won two elections with overwhelming white support while barely campaigning in black neighborhoods.[70] A majority of white voters supported both Rizzo and the dirty work necessary to maintain the city's racial order.

Can civilian review of police actions improve police-minority community relations? In the fifty years since the debates over civilian review boards first roiled American politics, police have become more militarized, and the war on drugs has further poisoned the relationship between police and minority communities.[71] Patterns of discriminatory policing, physical abuse, and violations of constitutional rights, according to Department of Justice investigations, remain commonplace in many police departments and in other sectors of the criminal justice system.[72] Even as police forces have become more diverse in terms of gender and race, aggressive policing remains the all-too-frequent first response to reports of crime or disorder. Scholars have noted that better training, more accountability, greater transparency, and the widespread acceptance of citizen and independent auditor reviews of citizen complaints have characterized most big-city police departments since the 1990s.[73] But, as recent events make clear, a strong current of dirty work continues to characterize the ways in which police interact with minority communities. If James Baldwin was right when he wrote "the only way to police a ghetto is to be oppressive,"[74] the limited possibilities of police reform are obvious.

## Chapter 5

# The Children's War

The years between 1965 and 1974 were among the city's bleakest. Philadelphia lost 40 percent of its industrial jobs in a single decade, and empty factories blighted the row-house neighborhoods that surrounded them. With jobs disappearing and hulking factory ruins subject to vandalism and arson scarring the neighborhoods, homeowners who could afford it abandoned the houses whose only virtue lay in their proximity to work. An average of five hundred people left the city each week, with the city's population decline in the 1970s greater than in any previous decade. Homicide rates, rising steadily since 1960, suddenly and catastrophically surged—by 300 percent between 1965 and 1974. The *Philadelphia Inquirer* dubbed 1969 "the year of the gun," as murder took white and black, female and male, old and young, but mostly young and black male lives. The most disheartening murders were those of adolescents killed in the city's spiraling youth gang conflicts. Gang-related deaths rose from about four per year in the early 1960s to forty-five in 1969, and their share of the city's homicides increased about sevenfold, from 2.4 percent in 1962 to 16.6 percent in 1969. And no one seemed to have a clue about what to do.[1]

James Tate and his police commissioner, Frank Rizzo, who followed Tate as mayor in 1972, were models of ineptitude. They ignored the city's fiscal problems, and Rizzo offered law-and-order bromides for its social issues. As police commissioner, Rizzo declared, "We're going to violate their [gang members] rights. They're going to be stopped and searched when they run in packs."[2] Police actions worsened relations with black youth, not only because of the constant harassment but also because the police deliberately exacerbated tensions between gangs by "turf dropping"—picking up gang members for questioning and then depositing them in their enemy's territory to hoof it home as best they could. When Rizzo ran for mayor, he did not campaign in black wards, and his incendiary appeals to white voters split the city.[3]

Community and church groups stepped into the vacuum left by divisive politicians and frequently maligned municipal agencies. They brokered truces between gangs, negotiated safe havens, involved gang members in community betterment projects, and appealed to racial solidarity to combat gang violence. Multiple initiatives failed multiple times as voluntary associations had few resources and fewer jobs to offer teenagers. But partial successes abounded and eventually dampened gang violence, at least until the underground economy emerged as a new and destructive employer of inner-city youth.

Of course Philadelphia, like other American cities, had always had gangs. In the nineteenth century, young men attached themselves to volunteer fire companies that were organized by ethnicity, religion, and neighborhood, and these companies battled each other as much as the blazes they were supposed to fight. Gangs participated in election battles, in enforcing neighborhood boundaries, especially against African Americans, and in general mayhem. But by the twentieth century, these traditions faded as professional fire services replaced volunteers in 1871, Protestant-Catholic rivalries cooled, a uniformed police force enforced order, and the city settled into decades of rule by a Republican political machine that obviated the need for pitched political battles.[4] Groups of adolescents colonized street corners, with their occasional fights sometimes leaving mangled and dead bodies, but in the decades before the 1960s, battles between armed groups were a thing of the distant past.

Race, demography, and technology combined in the 1960s to create a new social ecology that supported more frequent and deadlier gang conflicts. A declining white population should have opened new areas for African American settlement, but such transitions did not happen easily; so places where white and black settlements met were in near constant tension. Most of the gang rivalries were intraracial, however, as the surging black population was funneled into a handful of neighborhoods, and the sheer number of teenagers—the coming of age of the "baby boomers"—created the basis for increased conflict. The number of black males aged twelve to twenty-one went from about 37,000 in 1959 to approximately 66,800 in 1967. This created a "threshold effect": as more youths joined gangs, there was increasing pressure on others to do so in order to ensure safe passage even in one's home neighborhood. Some boys just "walked with" a gang ("walkies" who joined for protection but were otherwise inactive), while others "pulled with" them and readily joined in conflicts.[5]

When conflict loomed, gangs sometimes went on aggressive recruitment campaigns to beef up their numbers. While boys who were drafted into membership might not have been the most enthusiastic members, they had their own reasons for listening to the local gang's pitch. Boys who resided in a gang's territory faced being the victims of an attack just because of their residence, age, and gender; at least if they joined the local gang, they had support. As one former gang member put it, you had to belong to a gang "cause when you have no back-up out on the streets, it's like you're open game, because people don't have to fear repercussions." Yet sometimes, as in the case of sixteen-year-old Anthony Ames, the logic backfired. His parents claimed that Anthony refused to join either the Moroccos or their rival, the Seybert Street gang, and both gangs had beaten him up. Pressure by the gangs became so intense that he moved into his grandmother's house a few blocks away. But as he walked down the street with two Moroccos, a couple of Seybert Street boys pulled up in a car and fired a shotgun blast that killed Anthony.[6]

The gangs' organization reflected the number of boys in each neighborhood. The most common age-graded structure included peewees or midgets (eleven to fourteen years); juniors, sometimes called young boys (fifteen to eighteen); and old heads (older than eighteen), with the juniors doing most of the fighting. Leaders, known as "runners," together with the warlords, who were in charge of weapons and arranging fights, and the checkholders, who acted as advisors and emissaries to other gangs, formed the leadership and made decisions that others followed. Police identified twenty-seven active African American gangs and one white one in 1962, but just two years later, Mayor James Tate complained that forty-five gangs with two thousand members existed in one area alone, North Central Philadelphia, known colloquially as "the Jungle." In 1969, Police Commissioner Rizzo estimated that there were ninety-three organized gangs in the city, with a total membership of about 5,300. And the number continued to swell.[7]

The presence of so many gangs narrowed the possibility of movement for adolescents, making it virtually impossible for a youth to walk several blocks from his house because another gang would be only blocks away. The danger of crossing gang boundaries was such that, if a school principal could not negotiate a truce that marked the school as neutral territory and provided safe passage, kids simply stayed home. Sometimes one gang dominated a particular school, which imperiled rivals and nongang members alike. For example, Benjamin Franklin High School belonged to the Moroccos. As one parent explained, "Many kids who stay out would love to go back to school, but they're afraid to. If the Moroccos catch you, then you have a big fight."[8] In other instances, schools became battlegrounds contested by several rival groups. The Somerville gang, Germantown's largest, had around two hundred members, with the juniors attending Wagner Junior High School, which was located in the Clang gang's turf, and the older boys attending Germantown High School. The high school was situated in the Haines Street gang's turf, and members of another gang, the Brickyard, went there as well. With three rival gangs in attendance, clashes could break out at any time. And since both the Clang and Haines Street "owed bodies" to Somerville, which had lost one member to each gang the year before, the tension at both schools was palpable. As one youth said, "I think about dyin' every day."[9]

During the 1960s, gangs increased their firepower with predictable results. In the 1950s, gangs fought with fists, chains, bottles, car aerials, sticks, and occasionally, knives and homemade "zip guns," which were fashioned from a block of wood shaped like a pistol, with a portion of a car aerial serving as the barrel, and a nail powered by a thick rubber band as the firing pin. Clearly these weapons killed and maimed their targets, but over time guns became more available (nationally, handgun sales quadrupled between 1962 and 1968), and gang arsenals reflected the change. Police observed that virtually all gangs had access to a "corner gun," which was taken from its hiding place and passed from one youth to another when it was needed. Boys believed mistakenly that they were protected from prosecution in case of a shooting since the weapon could not be traced to a single owner. Commissioner Rizzo declared it was not "uncommon to confiscate pistols, revolvers, rifles, and shotguns" at a rumble.[10] In Philadelphia, homicide became the leading cause of death for young African American males in 1960, and the homicide rate for fifteen- to nineteen-year-old black males increased steadily thereafter, nearly quadrupling by 1975, from 42.6 per 100,000 in 1957–60, to 56.1 in 1961–65, to 105.8 in 1966–70, to 152.8 in 1971–75.[11] Death stalked the young in the streets of black Philadelphia.

Death came to seventeen-year-old Harry "Sunny" Leach one Sunday evening in October 1964, ironically as he was trying to arrange a peace conference. The shooting was the latest in a tit-for-tat pattern of conflict between the 23rd and Diamond Street gang that claimed the Raymond Rosen Homes as their turf and the nearby 21st and Norris Street boys. Toward the end of September, a fight between the gangs ended inconclusively or perhaps with a beating for 23rd and Diamond. At any rate, 23rd and Diamond felt the need to retaliate after the fight and later that night shot and wounded three 21st and Norris Street boys. Days later the Norris Street boys stormed into the Rosen project grounds and caught and stabbed one of their rivals. None of these incidents was reported in the press, and there is no evidence that they generated additional police patrols or other intervention efforts. Then on Sunday, October 10, word circulated that a couple of the Norris Street boys, Jim Boy and Butch, were in the barbershop at 23rd and Diamond getting their hair processed when several members of 23rd and Diamond went over to talk peace. The barbershop was apparently neutral turf, even though it was across the street from the Rosen homes, as boys from both gangs frequented it, and the boys assured the owner that there would be no trouble.

At the same time, another boy, Paul Phillips, reported that the 23rd and Diamond gang had the Norris Street boys cornered in the barbershop and that Jim Boy and Butch told him to "bring the piece." Several boys hurried to see George Randall, a twenty-one-year-old "old head," who had retreated from active gang life after turning eighteen, when any crime would be treated as an adult offense accompanied by adult time in prison. Apparently, Randall kept a rifle hidden on the roof of a shed behind his house, and the Norris Street boys retrieved the gun and handed it to sixteen-year-old Edward Fields. It is not clear whether this was a test to see if Fields would actually "burn" someone, or if Fields simply carried the gun and then got swept up in the adrenaline rush of a planned ambush of the gang's enemies.

Meanwhile Melvin Stokes, sixteen, a member of 23rd and Diamond, entered the barbershop with Sunny Leach and several other members to talk with Butch and Jim Boy. They agreed they would talk some more about a truce, and they started to head out. Sunny led the way while Melvin stopped for a moment to reassure Mr. King, the barber, that there would be no trouble.

Approaching the barbershop, Fields and the others saw Sunny Leach step out of the front door. Someone yelled "don't shoot," but it was too late: Fields had already hoisted the rifle and fired a single bullet that tore through the upper half of Sunny Leach's left eye, entering the skull through the opening for the left optic nerve and lodging in his brain. Since gangs tended to parcel out their bullets carefully, making target practice a luxury, it is likely that Fields's head shot was just the product of (ill) luck.

Following the shooting, the Norris Street boys all ran in different directions and one hid the rifle in an abandoned house on Norris Street. Melvin Stokes ran out of the barbershop, went over to Leach's body, and took a .22 caliber pistol from his coat pocket, not willing to leave one of the gang's prized pieces behind for the police to confiscate. Stokes took the pistol to the dead boy's sister's apartment and hid it under a pillow on the sofa.

The decisions about where to store weapons reflected the different neighborhood ecologies of the gangs. For the Norris Street boys, their blocks offered a number of abandoned houses and vacant lots in which to hide something. For Diamond Street, Stokes had to find a spot in someone's apartment in one of the high-rises. Guns were precious possessions that boys carefully stored away from the prying eyes of parents or the search warrants carried by police.

Police arrived quickly at the scene of Leach's murder and, through the juvenile gang unit, rounded up and interrogated some fifty youths before arresting Fields. Fields was old enough to be tried as an adult, and he pled guilty to second-degree murder, receiving a ten- to twenty-year sentence. He later appealed his conviction, but the Pennsylvania Supreme Court upheld it in 1975.[12]

Gangs in Philadelphia most frequently named themselves after their street corners rather than adopting the more fanciful names commonly found in New York City gangs. In fact, most youths said they belonged to a corner rather than to a gang.[13] Although there were Moroccos, the Moon gang, the Mighty Motherfuckers, and the Zulu Nation, among others, names such as 23rd and Diamond provided a more precise definition of identity and loyalty. Corner names indicated the microscopic nature of turf in the crowded neighborhoods of North Philadelphia. In the case of 23rd and Diamond and 21st and Norris, only five blocks separated the two groups' corners, but the presence of the Raymond Rosen homes, a grouping of eight thirteen-story towers that loomed over nearby row houses and disrupted the small-scale nature of the neighborhood, accentuated the differences between them. The development supported a dense network of youths in the project who aligned with one another against adolescents in the surrounding area. The Raymond Rosen homes created a break in the landscape, as did public housing projects elsewhere in the city, that shaped the formation of rival social identities.[14]

Areas undergoing racial transition became flashpoints for gang conflict. Even if these clashes accounted only for a minority of gang-related killings, they drew disproportionate attention. The Dirty Annies, a white gang in the Southwest Philadelphia neighborhood of Kingsessing, took its name from the candy store where they hung out, and parents encouraged them to resist the incursion of African Americans into the area. As a *Philadelphia Inquirer* reporter noted, "Most of them say flatly they don't like blacks and neither do their parents." The Annies claimed they had ceded one corner after the next as well as their old playground, which they said was taken over by blacks "who beat them up if they try to play there." Others claimed that they had been threatened with guns, something the *Inquirer* reporter verified. While he was interviewing the Annies, a car stopped for a light, and a black youth on the passenger side mimicked pointing a gun. "For a second I couldn't tell for sure whether it was a comb or gun, so I ducked out of the way, expecting a blast. But nothing happened and the auto took off." One boy said plaintively, "White parents are starting to realize they've got to help us out. We're the last white gang." Although the Annies claimed to be aggrieved, tragedy struck multiple times in its usual tit-for-tat fashion, with two African American youths and one white youth dying over several months in a set of skirmishes across the color line. These incidents continued for another decade and included the murder of one African American youth and the wounding of two others by snipers posted on a warehouse roof.[15]

Rivalries between African American gangs also lasted decades and involved a succession of individual participants. The Valley Gang, an amalgam of about a dozen corner gangs that joined together against outside threats, had the 21st and Norris Street gang (involved in Sunny Leach's murder) as its chief rival. One of the Valley's affiliates was the 25th and Diamond gang that had inherited the Rosen Homes as its domain and made the recreation center at 25th and Diamond its property. Gang wars had raged in the area since the 1950s, and at a peace conference one observer noted that the conflict had gone on for so many years that most participants no longer knew how it had started. Over fourteen months beginning in January 1974, eight young men were killed in the area as snipers took up positions in abandoned houses, and four children were wounded at a bus stop when a car filled with Norris Street boys drove into the Valley firing a twelve-gauge shotgun out the window. A week later two Norris Street boys were shot and killed in separate incidents.[16]

Drive-by shootings and sniping represented new and deadlier tactics. The old-fashioned rumble, where gangs faced each other in a free-for-all on a street corner or in a schoolyard, largely disappeared by the late 1960s in the face of better and more numerous arms. Gangs skirmished in groups of three or four, stole a car for a sortie designed to pick off an unwary adolescent, or on rare occasions invaded rivals' homes. Generally, grown-ups had been considered off limits in the past, but even that changed. Members of the 11th and Indiana gang got into a dispute with Joseph Brundage, who was driving a car full of children home from a municipal swimming pool. They asked Brundage for a lift, but he said he had no room. When he started to drive off, they jumped on the hood and the back of the car, falling to the ground as he drove. The gang wanted revenge and went looking for Brundage, and while they did not find him, they did see his cousin and fired two shots at him. When he disappeared into his house, several members kicked in the door and fired a shot into the chest of a sleeping twenty-seven-year-old woman, whose nine-year-old son was playing on the floor nearby.[17] Although home invasions and murders of adults remained uncommon, they added to the anxiety of a city fed up with gangs and murder. State Representative Hardy Williams, in a mass meeting of concerned parents at West Philadelphia High School, called gang violence "our own Vietnam in our own streets and the most persistent, terrifying and urgent problem this city faces."[18]

The police department's Juvenile Aid Bureau (JAD) had the job of controlling street gang activity. But as a division of the police, the JAD was widely mistrusted and participated in some of the worst abuses committed by police. Although the Gang Control Unit of the JAD frequently knew the names and addresses of gang members and used this information to find suspects after an incident, such intelligence came at a cost. Parents and community activists criticized the police for their policy of arresting every juvenile in sight, arguing that mass arrests, such as the ones following the Sunny Leach murder, just embittered youths, especially given their treatment ("they will pick up these boys and they will beat their heads in"). Arrestees, bound in tight handcuffs, were put in the back of police wagons and given a "rough ride" over Philadelphia's bumpy streets, getting bounced from side to side until they arrived at the precinct. Youths also blamed police for deliberately worsening relations between gangs. Gangs frequently clashed over rumors that circulated through the neighborhood, and one gang youth told a Crime Commission hearing that police "come up and tell us a wild story that the other gang told them, and they go down and tell the other gang what we said, and that is what causes trouble." Helen Frye, whose nine-year-old son had been shot to death while coming home after putting air in his bicycle tires, asked why police could not establish some sort of rapport with kids: "Maybe if the police had become better friends instead of making the boys afraid and angry, some of this could have been prevented." Parents also believed that police ignored reports that might have forestalled some violence. When told by members of the 16th and Wallace Street gang that the rival Moroccos had guns, "police got back in their car and kept heading on." One woman commented bitterly that after a gang shooting, police thought "that's just another nigger dead."[19] Whether or not most police actually felt that way was less important than the community members' conviction that they did.

More than any other practice, turf dropping aroused the most ire, especially after a youth was murdered after police left him in a rival gang's turf. Police picked up Norman Martin and two other members of the 8th and Oxford gang for questioning and then deposited them in the territory of 9th and Diamond Street, their periodic rivals. While Commissioner Rizzo never acknowledged police brutality nor responded to the complaints of community groups about turf dropping, which he termed "inadvertent" in Martin's case, he nonetheless ordered police to return youths to where they were first picked up. Despite Rizzo's orders, turf dropping continued.[20]

Philadelphia, like other cities confronted with gang problems, funded street workers to make contact with gangs, but the city's efforts were poorly coordinated and ineffective. The job included creating rapport with gang members, diverting them from conflict, finding recreational opportunities for them, and encouraging individuals to leave the gang and return to school or find employment. It was a dangerous and poorly paid job. The best street workers were former gang members with "street cred," something usually not acquired in college classrooms, and yet the Department of Public Welfare, which took over direct services to gangs in 1973, required that street workers have college degrees. Municipal street workers worked a nine-to-five day and had weekends off, which took them off the streets at precisely the times when youths got into trouble. Mayor Tate cut a request to fund a hundred additional gang workers from the Welfare Department's budget in 1970, at the height of the murders, and Mayor Rizzo's director of youth services was a political crony who was widely criticized for ineffectiveness. While all of this eventually changed—it made headlines when the city's Youth Conservation Services began to work weekends in 1970—it meant that city government's efforts to divert gangs from conflict left a large vacuum for many years, even as the gang problem worsened.[21]

Frank Rizzo's move into City Hall in 1972 did nothing to improve the situation. Although he had pledged to crack down on gangs, it quickly became apparent that his law-and-order approach produced few results. An editorial in the *Philadelphia Bulletin* noted that while the gang problem was no worse under Rizzo, "it's not better, either, in spite of his campaign pledge that 'we're going to move against these groups and not take any nonsense . . . they're going to be stopped.'"[22] The mayor responded that the gang problem could not be solved in his lifetime, and gang killings could not be stopped even if there were a policeman on every corner. He then called for more of the same: mass arrests of gang members, strict enforcement of curfew laws, stopping and searching groups of adolescents, outlawing anyone older than eighteen from belonging to a gang, and the elimination of bail in cases involving lethal violence, but the City Council—

more moderate in its views than the mayor—rejected his proposals as being unconstitutional.[23] City government simply could not figure out what to do. One fifth-grade student at Walton Elementary School captured the frustration of the city when he wrote, "If you can't do your job as Mayor of Philadelphia, then pack your bags and leave, because there are plenty of people who can take your place."[24]

In the absence of political leadership and effective municipal agencies, private groups—settlement houses, churches, community associations, and concerned parents—stepped into the breach. Such groups had been working with street gangs since the 1930s, when conflict among African American gangs first emerged. Samuel Evans organized the North Philadelphia Youth Movement in 1937 and created "Youth City" in the area east of Broad Street. The Wharton Centre, named after Susan Parrish Wharton, a pioneering social worker, began outreach in the area west of Broad in the 1940s after a series of shootings, and the center organized Operation Street Corner, which by 1953 had 350 former gang members organized into 14 clubs. The project ended in 1958, when funding ran out, and gang warring remained an endemic part of the neighborhood despite the center's work.[25] The Wharton Centre's problems with funding were typical of private settlement and church groups, which had many other needs and clients to serve.

Both public and private agencies' work with gangs remained uncoordinated, and some of their efforts backfired. Having a street worker assigned gave a gang status: they were so bad that they had to have a "man" assigned to them. Other gangs then had a perverse incentive to act out. An outreach worker's presence sometimes solidified gang membership inadvertently by offering services or resources that were otherwise unavailable. The Crime Prevention Association, which provided outreach workers under a municipal contract, worked with the 12th and Oxford gang and helped them form the 12th and Oxford Film-Makers Corporation. With advice and technical assistance, the gang produced a widely shown semidocumentary, *The Jungle*, about gang life in North Philadelphia. Gang members learned to use cameras and editing equipment, some worked on the screenplay, others as actors—and they were paid a dollar an hour for their work. Once the film was finished, the group traveled to other cities, including Los Angeles, to promote it. As a sign of their transformation, some began getting tutored in English and mathematics at Temple University, and the City Planning

Commission hired several youths to help teach commission members more about the neighborhoods in North Philadelphia. The 12th and Oxford Corporation also received a grant from the Printing Progress Club to set up a printmaking operation in the basement of their headquarters, and the Philadelphia Gas Works (PGW) provided a loan to open a laundromat that would serve the neighborhood and provide a source of employment.[26]

As word got around, nearby gangs became jealous. Gang members stopped PGW trucks and asked, "When you going to do something for 8th and Diamond [12th and Oxford's main rival]?" Despite the time and investment by all these groups, Robert Nixon and James Ravenell, two of 12th and Oxford's leaders, were convicted of murdering Marvin Smith, whom Ravenell shot at point-blank range with a gun supplied by Nixon. One of the 12th and Oxford peewees had been "moved on" by 8th and Diamond, and the older boys felt honor bound to seek revenge. In a separate incident, the nineteen-year-old cameraman for the 12th and Oxford filmmakers, Garfield Peacock, was shot and killed while trying to arrange a treaty between the 12th and Oxford juniors and the neighboring Marshall and Master Street gang. One of his friends said of Peacock, "He got out of it. He wanted to do something for the community." But "getting out of it" was anything but easy; one did not simply walk away from one's gang reputation and shed old enmities, and the attempts by outside groups to aid in a gang's transformation could only go so far without addressing the needs of other gangs and the environment in which gang members lived.[27]

While it was possible both to turn an individual gang toward more "prosocial" activities and to negotiate treaties between warring gangs, such piecemeal efforts ran up against a larger tide of violence. Working with a single gang or even with several warring gangs could be undercut by the actions of one of the junior divisions that might want to preserve the fighting identity of the corporate entity or by another gang left out of the negotiations. Melvin Floyd, a police officer, Baptist minister, and former gang member, recounted that over twenty-one years there had been nineteen truces between the Moroccos and the Tenderloins. But a new killing broke each one.[28]

Civil rights and black power leaders used appeals to racial solidarity to get gangs to end their fighting. As early as 1964, the leader of the Philadelphia chapter of CORE, Louis Smith, got thirty members of the Valley Gang to go to Chester, Pennsylvania, to participate in a civil rights demonstra-tion. "These boys won't come with zip guns or knives. We've been working with them and they're coming along fine," Smith explained. And the fire-brand leader of Philadelphia's chapter of the NAACP, Cecil B. Moore, made repeated alliances with the notorious Moroccos, enlisting them to join the six months of protests demanding the opening of Girard College to African Americans. The all-white boarding school for fatherless boys, supported by banker and philanthropist Stephen Girard's trust, abutted the Morocco's Francisville neighborhood.[29] The Moroccos participated in a "lie-in" that stopped traffic on Girard Avenue and formed a "freedom train" picket line in which they ran in a circle outside the main gate of the school taunting the police: "If I had a low IQ, I'd be a policeman too," and more ominously, "Jingle bells, shotgun shells, freedom all the way; oh what fun it is to blast a bluecoat bigot away." When a more moderate group of members chal-lenged Moore's leadership of the Philadelphia NAACP, he brought a group of Moroccos with him to the convention to demonstrate his support among the common folk. Then Moore organized about 150 gang youths to declare a truce and go out in six sound trucks and on foot to promote a voter registration drive in support of black political power. No doubt Moore's confrontational politics, his willingness to defy police and stand up to "The Man," and his work as a tenacious criminal defense lawyer all earned him the respect and loyalty of the Moroccos.[30]

Yet even as the Moroccos marched for civil rights and organized voters, they plotted against their long-standing rivals, the Tenderloins and the 16th and Wallace Street gang. Lorenzo King and Saxton Boykin were held with-out bail for the killing of Willie Lewis Bingham of 16th and Wallace because the district attorney feared the two Moroccos would be murdered if not kept in custody. In another incident, three Moroccos were shot when they crossed into Tenderloin turf.[31] Fighting for civil rights did not preclude other forms of combat, especially in the absence of similar commitments from rival gangs.

The Black Panther Party also recruited gang members to join their ranks. What historian Matthew Countryman has called its "hypermascu-line" rhetoric and appeal to self-defense resonated with gang members used to defying authority and battling police. Reggie Schell, a former gang mem-ber and veteran, helped organize the first Black Panther Party chapter in

Philadelphia, becoming its defense captain in 1969. Schell brought gang members into several protests against police brutality and for better city services in their neighborhoods. For three nights in August 1971, Schell got gang members to collect and burn trash and overturn abandoned cars to draw the city's attention to lack of trash collection and car removal in North Philadelphia. Schell, then representing the Black United Liberation Front, organized a dozen gangs into a coalition by arguing that their real enemies were not other gang members but the establishment. "Why are you dudes killing each other?" he asked in a question that must have occurred to others. "Black people must unite for self-determination."[32]

The Nation of Islam, with its strong presence in the nation's prisons, also began recruiting gang members and providing them with an ideological alternative to gangs. When former inmates returned to their neighborhoods, they advised younger gang members to stop their fratricidal fighting. As one youth said, "Many of the old heads have joined the Nation and their philosophy doesn't tolerate gang warring." Like the Panthers, the Nation of Islam benefited from the masculinist appeal inherent in its resistance to police and a white-dominated power structure.[33]

In efforts too numerous to mention, black nationalist groups, ministers, and community organizations arranged peace treaties among gangs and tried to engage young people in a sense of larger purpose.[34] Many succeeded for a time before crumbling in the face of unremitting gang rivalry or personal animosities that could not be overcome. The gang credo was a body for a body—not turn the other cheek—and the emphasis on armed self-defense, on resisting the establishment, and on a virulent masculinity by many militant groups, while understandable in the social context of the time, threatened to feed rather than quell the violence in the streets.

But then something happened. By the mid-1970s the tide turned, homicide rates dropped, and gang murders nearly disappeared. While forty-three gang-related deaths occurred in 1973, in 1974 the total fell to thirty-three. In 1975 it was fifteen; in 1976 it fell to six. A permanent citywide gang truce, negotiated first in 1972, when it lasted for sixty days, became the focus for community groups: "No Gang War in '74" and "Keep More Alive in '75" became the slogans heard in neighborhoods around the city. Sister Falaka Fattah and the House of Umoja were its engineers.[35]

Falaka Fattah (née Frankie Davenport), mother of six boys and living in a gang-filled South Philadelphia neighborhood, became an antigang activist out of necessity. Fattah was a journalist and a black power activist who had participated in the Black Panther Party's Revolutionary People's Constitutional Convention in 1970. She wanted to understand why black youths were killing each other in gang wars and asked her husband, David, to do some investigatory research. His findings quickly became personal. Their sixteen-year-old son Robin had become a player in the Clymer Street gang, and she and David resolved to intervene. Not only did they confront Robin in a family meeting, but they also invited the family members of the Clymer Street gang to a group meeting at their house. Her proposal was startling: they would sell their house and move to a new African-themed residence in West Philadelphia, far from the Clymer Street gang rivals, and any of the other gang members were free to move with them. Ultimately fifteen of them did so, and the House of Umoja was born.[36]

The House of Umoja (a Swahili word meaning *unity*) emphasized membership in an extended family, personal responsibility, shared work, time management, commitment to community norms, and conflict resolution, all clothed in African-inspired ritual. Residents promised to give up gang fighting as a condition for joining, and those who stayed were considered "sons" and the brothers of Fattah's own children. As Falaka Fattah explained, "Some stayed for a night, some for a week, and some stayed for years," and those who made a successful transition were invited to adopt the Fattah surname. David Fattah tutored residents in math, while Falaka taught journalism and presided over the Adella, the weekly community meetings, which were a combination of consensus building and self-criticism. The House of Umoja accepted court and reformatory referrals, who eventually comprised about half the house members, and individuals charged with any crime except for sexual offenses. The house maintained an open-door policy—even for those referred by the criminal justice system—since voluntary commitment to the Umoja philosophy was considered the key to individual reform.[37]

The original house on Frazier Street was too small for the Fattahs, their children, and the expanding number of gang members who sought refuge there. When the Clymer Street gang moved in, the Fattahs removed all the furniture in the four-room house to make way for mattresses. "All we promised was to help them stay alive and out of jail," said Fattah. After a year, all were alive and none were in jail, and "as word spread, members of other gangs began seeking sanctuary at the house." The Fattahs acquired additional houses on the block through pooling resources; donations from church, business, and community groups; and a partnership with Bell Telephone. By 1972, they had painted eight houses in the red, green, and black colors of African liberation, and by 1977 they had taken over twenty houses on the block, all maintained by the youths themselves. The goal was a "black boys' town" with a security patrol and escort service for neighborhood residents and a free school for local children.[38]

The model of having representatives of different gangs negotiating and working cooperatively gave rise to the first Umoja-sponsored gang truce in 1972. Mayor Rizzo had given gangs an ultimatum: turn in weapons with no questions asked, or face a relentless routine of stops and body frisks wherever they were sighted by police. The gang members living in Umoja thought that no one would turn in guns voluntarily, especially to Frank Rizzo's police, but they might agree not to use them. They suggested getting the gangs together to negotiate a citywide truce, and they put on the house blackboard the names of the gangs to invite to the summit, which was held in the Friends 4th Street Meeting House on February 9, 1972. Some five hundred gang members attended and signed an Imani (faith) pact to end the street wars. Participants agreed to meet again in March to reaffirm the pact. In the meantime, they agreed to smaller meetings to resolve any disputes. As Falaka Fattah said, "There was a consensus . . . that there would no longer be killing of black people by black people."[39]

Although the follow-up summit did occur in early April 1972, and some sixty gangs attended with the goal of having a United High Council of Gangs, the two summits only brought about sixty days of peace. Within several weeks, the Valley Gang and 21st and Norris were at it again, with over a hundred youths from 21st and Norris rampaging through the Raymond Rosen homes after attending a funeral for one of their members. The city tallied a discouraging thirty-eight gang-related deaths in 1972, and the number climbed to forty-three the following year, about the same number as in 1969. As Fattah put it, the gangs became "restless," and the early talks were not followed up. In response, Fattah announced a new effort in November 1973 to have a citywide conference on January 1, where the gangs would agree to a New Year's resolution: No Gang Wars in '74 and "hopefully forever."[40]

The Fattahs planned this larger summit meticulously. David Fattah visited imprisoned gang members to secure their support for the peace pledge. While it was too late for these men, it was not too late for their younger brothers, cousins, and friends, and the prisoners put out word of their support and suggested the names of invitees. The Committee of Black Clergymen asked all black ministers to make gang warring a topic for their services on Sunday, December 30, and to encourage youths to participate in the summit. In addition to renewing the Imani pledge, gangs negotiated individual treaties, including one between the Valley and 21st and Norris gangs. Some 475 gang members representing 32 gangs along with community members and politicians attended the nine-hour conference. Gang members agreed to sell T-shirts with Falaka Fattah's face and the slogan "No Gang War in '74" for five dollars each. Participants also agreed that youths wearing the shirts were off-limits regardless of where they traveled in the city, and Umoja used the proceeds from the sale of T-shirts to fund other activities.[41]

Falaka Fattah was a tireless and imaginative promoter. She traveled to Harrisburg, where she persuaded Governor Milton Shapp to approve placing "no gang war" posters in all the state liquor stores in Philadelphia. She organized a seven-hour "Life-a-Thon" broadcast on WDAS, a black-oriented radio station, with two hundred volunteers in the field working to have gang members sign the pledge and then phoning the results to the station. Fattah explained, "We didn't ask them to stop fighting, just merely to pledge not to kill. Not to get a body, whenever there is a confrontation." In order to promote black political power in the city, workers from the House of Umoja traveled to playgrounds, nightclubs, and other gathering places to register voters, with results reported in a "Vote-a-Thon" on WKDU-FM. In 1976, she organized a black youth Olympics that pitted contestants from Philadelphia against ones from Boston as part of the bicentennial celebration.[42] But publicity and voting drives were not enough; above all, Fattah knew that in order to maintain the peace pledge she had to involve parents.

Mothers' marches became a fixture in Philadelphia in the mid-1970s. Lieutenant Willie Williams of the Gang Control Unit credited the involvement of parents, especially mothers, noting, "Mothers marched in the streets. That was effective because they knew the kids would not shoot their own mothers."[43] Jean Hobson formed the North Philadelphia Mothers Concerned, who armed themselves with broomsticks and mop handles and took over a gang corner, giving notice that they would not be intimidated and would sweep gangs out of the neighborhood. As the group expanded, it headed to hot spots in Philadelphia with bands of roving pickets carrying signs stating "Stop the Killing" and "Save the Children." One mother explained, "We found our gang members were our own children. We didn't know the names of the gangs. We know we have them now." They also posted people on street corners to watch out for trouble and to call police if necessary. As one report concluded, "Since the initial mothers group was organized two years ago, the area has been transformed from one of the city's most violent into a livable neighborhood."[44]

The maternalist politics of Falaka Fattah and Mothers Concerned counteracted the masculinist posture of the Panthers and other revolutionary groups. Fattah was no less nationalist and no less willing to confront injustices than other Afrocentrists, but her focus was on using Afrocentric forms to stop violence by building bridges across different communities. The mothers' marches were less ideological but used mothers' concerns to confront and disrupt gang activity. Their presence on the street deliberately interrupted the pattern of attack and retribution that had characterized gang violence, and they forced gang members to recognize the pain caused by their actions. Fattah and Mothers Concerned stepped in where the state was ineffective and demanded attention from local youth while also pressuring city government to fulfill its responsibilities for public safety. Like other female-led community antipoverty and welfare rights groups active at the time, they lobbied for the extension of basic civil and social rights that other communities took for granted.[45]

It would be misleading, however, to claim that only maternal and community efforts turned the tide; rather, a combination of factors led to the decline in gang killings. Certainly, the citywide gang truce addressed the problem of piecemeal negotiations between separate gangs that scuttled earlier efforts at peace. The United Council of Gangs met regularly to resolve disputes during 1974, with special emergency meetings when a confrontation between gangs seemed imminent. As one member of the 12th and Poplar gang said, "There's still some fighting like at dances. But usually we can control it in a day or two. We've got a way to communicate now." More effective gang intervention work by the city also helped. Six million dollars in federal money reinvigorated city efforts by putting five six-member teams into the field, allowing gang workers, such as Bennie Swans and his Crisis Intervention Network, to flood areas in anticipation of trouble.[46] This combination of efforts pushed gangs below the threshold where boys no longer felt vulnerable if they did not belong. Gangs did not disappear, but there were fewer of them; and gang wars occurred with decreasing frequency and diminishing casualties.

There were two other factors beyond anyone's control that also contributed to the decline in gang violence. One was demographic: just as the surge in adolescent males in the mid-1960s swelled the number of boys in the prime age groups for joining gangs, a modest decline in their number made fewer recruits available. Between 1970 and 1980, the number of ten-to- seventeen-year-old males in Philadelphia declined by slightly more than 20 percent. So at the same time that community efforts depressed gang violence, the number of potential members was also diminishing.[47]

Heroin was the second factor. Public officials, editors, and community activists all described a steady increase in heroin use in the same neighborhoods where gangs were present. Philadelphians warily eyed events in New York, where gangs had largely disappeared only to be replaced by heroin users. Gangs had generally shunned heroin users, who were unreliable fighters and who needed to cross gang boundaries in order to score both money and drugs. But heroin gradually made inroads, especially as gang fighting, with its demands for vigilance and tight organization, diminished; a raid on the Zulu Nation headquarters uncovered "a large quantity of hypodermic needles" and other drug paraphernalia, while the eight suspects arrested all had fresh track marks. White gangs in the poor river wards had always been less organized than the African American gangs, and the increase in their heroin use was particularly noticeable. The former Panther Reggie Schell said, "Most of the young guys now are hustling dope . . . so they don't have time to just kill for nothing [gang fighting]. They kill you for your money."[48]

The House of Umoja became a favorite of Reagan-era conservatives, and as president, Ronald Reagan pointed to David and Falaka Fattah as an example of what voluntarism and family values could accomplish. "I wish the cynics would visit David and Falaka Fattah," Reagan said. "This is one couple that have done what all the social welfare and law enforcement organizations have been unable to accomplish. They have replaced the gang structure with the family structure."[49] Certainly their accomplishments and those of other parents and community and religious groups deserve to be lauded. Few matched their dedication to delinquent adolescents and their ability to think imaginatively to gain publicity and to enlist allies in the battle against youth violence. And yet neither the Fattahs nor Ronald Reagan had an answer for the black youth unemployment rate, estimated at 60 percent, that underpinned gang violence.[50] When Reagan axed the federal program that supplied gang workers for the city, the number of city workers, including street workers employed under the Comprehensive Employment and Training Act (CETA), fell from a high of 4,442 in 1978 to none in 1987. The federal share of Philadelphia's municipal budget fell from 6 percent in 1974 to 0.5 percent in 1987 as Philadelphia and cities across the nation were gutted by supply-side economics and Reagan-era tax cuts for the wealthy.[51] The market eventually did supply inner-city youth with jobs—via the drug trade—and murder rates began to soar once more.

Chapter 6

# Street Wars

## Shooting Police and Police Shootings

The most difficult weekend in Philadelphia's history of policing began on Saturday, August 29, 1970. That night, six Black Unity Council members ambushed and killed Sergeant Frank Von Colln in an isolated Cobbs Creek Park guardhouse, and then wounded Officer James Harrington as he and his partner drove up.[1] The next day, August 30, amid an intense citywide search for the shooters, Officer Thomas Gibbons Jr., the son of the former police commissioner, and Officer John Nolan were making a car stop near Cobbs Creek Park when the two occupants suddenly opened fire as the officers approached the vehicle. The two shooters were not revolutionaries but rather burglars who had stolen guns and a car, but since the shooting happened in the same neighborhood, at first it seemed potentially related.[2] Finally, three officers suffered gunshot wounds in battles that erupted on Monday, after Police Commissioner Frank Rizzo ordered raids on three Black Panther headquarters in retaliation for Saturday's ambush of the police. That raised to seven the number of officers shot in a thirty-six-hour period.[3] Police in Philadelphia were fighting a street war, and the streets were fighting back.

Policing was never a safe profession, though in terms of per capita casualty rates, it ranked far below the more hazardous occupations of mining, farming, and construction.[4] In Philadelphia, intentional killings of police officers averaged about five per decade during the 1950s and 1960s, with additional officers dying in car or motorcycle accidents, in falls, or from heart attacks while on duty. In total, intentional killings of police accounted for one-third of the police deaths that occurred in these decades. Then, in the 1970s, the number of police killed by civilians increased dramatically. Intentional killings, such as the ambush of Frank Von Colln, soared to nineteen, or about two-thirds of the twenty-nine police deaths that decade.[5] Clearly, policing had become considerably more dangerous.

At the same time, police killings of civilians, usually classified as justifiable homicides, increased in similar fashion. Police in Philadelphia killed an average of about 3 civilians per year during the 1950s—32 in total between 1950 and 1960.[6] Between 1960 and 1970, police killed 80 Philadelphians, slightly more than 7 per year, or more than double the average of the previous decade. The shooting victims included 59 African Americans and one Puerto Rican, or two-thirds of the total, and 20 whites, with the overwhelming majority of the killings (92 percent) deemed justifiable.[7] Then, between 1970 and 1978, police shootings of civilians more than doubled again as Philadelphia police killed 162 civilians, an average of 18 deaths per year; about two-thirds of the victims were Latino or African American. In many instances, police fired their weapons in confrontations where the use of force could in no way be justified, and yet there were few if any legal consequences. About half of the 469 total police shootings between 1970 and 1978 appeared to be contrary to Pennsylvania law, which was changed in 1973 to eliminate the common law "fleeing felon" standard that had allowed police to use deadly force to stop, for example, an unarmed and fleeing burglar. The new standard allowed the use of deadly force only when an officer's life or that of another person was in danger or to prevent the escape of a violent felon when other means of apprehension had failed. Yet, according to a study by the Public Interest Law Center of Philadelphia, 75 of those shot and 17 of those killed had not committed a violent crime, were unarmed at the time of their shooting, and apparently were retreating from police, making these killings clearly in violation of Pennsylvania law.[8] But there were no repercussions for police—at least in terms of the criminal justice system.

My argument here is that the killing of police officers and the police killing of civilians were mutually reinforcing, part of the social ecology of violence that shaped so many Philadelphia neighborhoods. According to contemporary studies, community-level violence and homicide in particular are associated with police use of deadly force. Simply put, police shoot more readily when they patrol in a community with high levels of violence and where they approach individuals with the expectation that they might be armed and dangerous.[9] During the 1970s, members of the black community were not only shooting back when stopped by police but also initiating violence, while police in turn were killing more civilians.[10] Across the nation, the intentional killing of police reached an all-time high during the 1970s, reflecting the fractured nature of American society during the decade, and Philadelphia epitomized the violent conflict between police and minority communities.[11] What linked the intentional killing of police and the murder of civilians in Philadelphia was the aggressive pattern of policing inaugurated by Police Commissioner Frank Rizzo. During his two terms as mayor, fatal shootings by police increased by about 20 percent per year.[12] Rizzo's policies, first as police commissioner and then as mayor, heightened tensions between police and minority communities to an even greater degree than in the past and produced the increasingly deadly interactions that characterized Philadelphia in this decade.

The year 1970 was bad even before the assassination of Frank Von Colln. On January 30, a young police officer, Frederick Cione, with less than a year on the force, was found shot to death on a North Philadelphia street. Cione's patrol car was parked in the middle of the street, with the driver's side door open, the motor running, and the lights on, while Cione lay ten feet away with two bullets in his chest, his service revolver still in its holster. According to the last entry in his log book, Cione made a pedestrian stop at 1:00 a.m., about seven minutes before someone called police with the report of gunshots being fired. Eyewitness accounts were contradictory, with several reporting that two or three men had sped away in a car that was parked behind Cione's patrol car. Other accounts disputed this, and the information in Cione's log and the position of the body make it seem improbable that he had made a car stop. Several residents claimed that they saw three men run around the corner and flee on foot following the shooting. The most detailed account came from a young woman on her way home, who said that Cione had stopped three young African American men, two of whom had moved against a wall ready to be frisked, while the third turned suddenly toward Cione and shot him twice at point-blank range.[13]

Police responded to the shooting in their usual fashion—by blanketing the neighborhood with officers and randomly rounding up young men for questioning. As part of "Operation Find," police detained over a thousand black men living in the vicinity of 17th and Oxford Streets, where Cione's patrol car was found. The intent was to apply such pressure on the community that someone would eventually come forward with information about Cione's murder. Instead, Operation Find eventually led to the filing of a civil suit against the City of Philadelphia that accused the city of condoning the routine violation of black citizens' constitutional rights.[14]

The experiences of Frank Alexander and Marvin Terry, two of the plaintiffs in the suit, illustrate the harassment faced by youths in the area, both immediately following the shooting and over the next several months. The pair was first arrested on January 30, right after the incident. Police told them to get up against the wall, spread-eagled and ready to be searched. Following the search, police brought them downtown to the Roundhouse, the Philadelphia Police Department's headquarters, where they were detained in a room with some two hundred other men for five hours of questioning. Commissioner Rizzo appeared and ordered the police to obtain names, addresses, and photographs of each individual before releasing them.

Police stopped Alexander and Terry again the next day as they walked on Broad Street. Police spread-eagled and searched them before putting them in the wagon for transport to district headquarters. Officers told them that "police were arresting for investigation about the death of Officer Cione every young man who they saw wearing a black leather jacket." Alexander and Terry explained that they had already been arrested, detained, and questioned, and after police confirmed the story, the pair was released.

Police detained Alexander and Terry for the third time on February 3. Police arrived at their homes, but finding neither suspect there, officers left messages for the two to surrender themselves at the Roundhouse the next evening. When Alexander and Terry showed up, police held them for eight hours of intense questioning and gave them lie-detector tests before allowing them to go home.

On February 12, around 3:00 a.m., a force of shotgun-toting police burst into Alexander's home without a search warrant and hauled him out for another round of questioning—the fourth in a two-week period. Simultaneously, another group of police raided Terry's home, where his terrified family assured police that he was not there but they would get him to surrender. Police told Terry's mother that her son should surrender as soon as possible because "we want him and he might get hurt." After Terry turned himself in, police handcuffed Terry and Alexander to chairs and beat them around the head, while relays of detectives questioned them for the next twenty-three hours before releasing them without charges. Alexander was arrested for a fifth time on March 6. Elizabeth Alexander, Frank's mother, complained, "I know this sort of harassing treatment isn't just happening to only Frank, it just happens all the time. . . . This is not new treatment; black people have been indiscriminately picked up for years." In a similar vein, Lucille Terry, Marvin's mother, said, "I just get the feeling that the police do as they want, arrest people or pat them down on the street and never tell them why or what for. After a while you just let them do as they want or you know you'll get hurt. Everything gets worse when a policeman gets injured or killed and no one has any rights." Lucille Terry concluded that police had been acting this way for years, and "then they wonder why no one will cooperate with them."[15]

And no one did cooperate with them. Despite the many arrests and the raids on people's homes, Frederick Cione's murder remained unsolved—the only intentional killing of a police officer in Philadelphia that has never been cleared. Raids, mass arrests, and a general disregard for constitutional rights were standard practices in the wake of a police officer's murder as police locked down entire communities in their zeal to find the killer of one of their own.[16] Not only did police want to pressure a community for information; they also needed to reassert their control over the community, to show young men, in particular, who was in charge of the streets.

These actions only further exacerbated the already hostile environment in which police patrolled, making future confrontations inevitable. In response to police actions, Community Legal Services filed a civil suit against Frank Rizzo and top police officers in the name of the city's 750,000 black residents. The suit alleged that the mass detentions of black North Philadelphians were not just a response to Cione's murder but in fact were "common-place in all the city's black communities." Police acted as if the "homes, persons and lives [of black Philadelphians] are completely at the disposal and whim of the Philadelphia Police Department." The Council of Black Clergy rallied behind the lawsuit as black Philadelphians of all classes rejected the oppressive tactics of the police department.[17] Police and community members, especially the young men most likely to be harassed by police, eyed each other with fear and hostility. And police expecting to encounter hostility and danger were more likely to use deadly force in a confrontation.

West Philadelphia's Black Unity Council organized against this backdrop of police repression and black resistance. First formed in 1967, the Black Unity Council aimed to stop drug use and sales, to prevent black street gangs from killing one another, and to protest police brutality. Like the Black Panthers with whom they later merged, the Unity Council provided food, distributed clothing, and staged cultural events for the neighboring community. The group became increasingly radicalized, reading Malcolm X and Marcus Garvey and studying Marx and capitalism as part of their self-education about the black experience in America. Over time, the original forty or so members dwindled to a hard core of six who were ready to start armed resistance. These six, according to the district attorney, rejected the Black Panthers as "too soft"; more likely, they were allied with the Panthers' underground and were part of an emerging number of black revolutionary groups that coalesced as the Black Liberation Army (BLA) and that decided to turn rhetoric into action.[18]

Where the Black Panther Party formed the aboveground faction that used its community programs to build public support for black political power and provided needed social services, the BLA was the loosely affiliated clandestine wing, dedicated to armed struggle and focused on attacking police as part of its defense of the black community. As Russell Shoats, a founder of the Black Unity Council and one of those convicted of Frank Von Colln's murder, put it in an essay written many years later, "Police officers were killed while they sat in their cars or directed traffic; this was war."[19]

Alvin Joyner, another of the Unity Council members who was convicted and sentenced to life imprisonment for Von Colln's murder, specifically cited police brutality and shootings of civilians as the impetus for the group's formation. He told police, "We became interested in everything that was happening to Black people in particular, also oppressed people of any color, you know, like the things happening in the Black community; the beatings of Blacks, the brutality, and the white business owner exploiting our people. About two or three weeks ago, we were discussing police brutality, such as Harold Brown. . . . We felt that people should arm themselves against these acts as self-defense."[20]

The handling of seventeen-year-old Harold Brown's shooting after a stolen car chase incensed many black Philadelphians in the spring of 1970. After Brown and two companions crashed the stolen car and fled the scene, he was shot fatally, allegedly after turning on Officer Brinley Evans with a knife. The medical examiner concluded that the shooting was justified, but Evans and his partner, Thomas Lyons, were charged with beating the youth as he lay dying on the street. When the officers were cleared of those charges as well, the Black Panthers issued wanted posters with the names and likenesses of Evans and Lyons, further upping the ante in an already tense city.[21]

As rhetoric about "offing the pigs" escalated, another police shooting on nearby 60th Street set the Black Unity Council into motion. Initially, they had decided to attack the local police precinct, but finding it impregnable, they turned to the Cobbs Creek park guard station instead. The six conspirators—Alvin Joyner, his brother Robert Joyner, Hugh Williams, Fred Burton, Russell Shoats, and Richard Thomas—met at a bar around 8:00 p.m. and finalized their plans. The Joyner brothers and Russell Shoats positioned themselves as lookouts, while the other three headed for the park guardhouse. The unexpected arrival of Officers Harrington and Kenner forced the lookouts into action, as Shoats waved down the car. James Harrington testified, "I turned to my partner and said something. I don't recall what. At this time, when I returned my head to see where this man was, there was a gun right in my face and a shot fired striking me here, exiting through the left rear of my neck. . . . I then fell forward in the wagon with blood, teeth, everything blocking my wind passage. I was having very great difficulty in breathing. I was . . . more or less laying on the floor of the wagon. At this time, I happened to look up and I saw my partner who was Henry Kenner . . . leaning across the wagon. I saw a flash from his gun. . . . I took my fingers and tried to clear my mouth so I could breathe and with this I lost sight of Henry Kenner. Then he came back and got me in a sitting position where I could breathe." Shoats, after exchanging shots with Kenner, took off in the other direction. Meanwhile, Alvin Joyner came out from behind a tree as the exchange of gunfire took place. "I thought I was being shot at and I took off." Joyner claimed never to have fired his weapon:

"I heard one shot, then I heard five or six other shots coming from the wagon, I'm not sure because I started running."[22]

Down at the guardhouse, the exchange of gunfire alerted officers Bradley and Massimo, who jumped into their car and raced up the hill, leaving Von Colln alone in the guardhouse. Several boys who had been playing ball in the park, and who had seen the exchange of gunfire between Shoats and the police, ran into the guardhouse, where Von Colln told them to hide for safety. As Von Colln talked on the phone in response to the assist-officer call, Richard Thomas, according to the prosecutor, walked into the guardhouse and pumped five bullets into Von Colln's back. (Thomas was arrested in Chicago in 1996 in a routine police stop and then extradited to Philadelphia. A jury found Thomas not guilty when his coconspirators refused to testify against him, which meant that their statements implicating him in the killing could not be introduced into evidence, and time-weakened memories made the other witnesses contradict themselves about the events of the night.)[23]

Meanwhile, police wagons converged at the site of the Harrington shooting, where the crime lab technicians were taking photographs and processing the scene. About twenty minutes later, an officer went down to the guardhouse to make a call and found Von Colln's body. Police arrested Hugh Williams as he left the park, with a hand grenade still in his possession, and he informed police that the group was supposed to rendezvous the next day. Only Robert Joyner showed up, and his arrest led in turn to the arrest of his brother and the recovery of a rifle and additional grenades, which were supposed to have been used to attack police as they arrived on the scene of the guardhouse shooting. Burton and Shoats were picked up later, while Thomas went on the lam. Marion Williams, Hugh Williams's wife, turned state's witness and provided details of the plotters' meeting in her home to plan killing police officers.[24]

The murders of Frederick Cione and Frank Von Colln suggest a range of motives behind the killing of police officers. The Von Colln murder was the clearly premeditated deed of an organized revolutionary group seeking to spur armed resistance to civil authority in the United States. One reason for the increase in intentional killings of police officers both in Philadelphia and nationally was the rise of violent revolutionary groups, such as the BLA and the Revolutionary Action Movement. Armed self-defense against white supremacist groups and the Ku Klux Klan had a long history as part of black resistance in the South, while challenging police harassment and monitoring police patrols became a central practice of the Black Panthers in the North and West. Underground groups, such as the Black Guards, an affiliate of the Revolutionary Action Movement, plotted to fight an urban guerrilla war while developing bases in the southern countryside from which Viet Cong–style raids could be launched. While most of this did not come to fruition, as many as twenty police deaths around the country were attributed to these groups, which in the 1970s began to ambush police officers, rob banks, and take other radical actions.[25]

Cione's killing, however, was more likely a spur-of-the-moment decision, similar to the incidents police faced in their ordinary patrol duties. It may have been an expression of the hostile relations between police and the communities they patrolled, but criminals frequently fired shots at police in an attempt to avoid arrest and incarceration. Such shootings did not have political motivations, even if the radical rhetoric of the time may have made such motivations more likely.

Other shootings seemed to fall in between these two poles: not the product of an overtly political group but more than a random violent encounter between a cop and a criminal. When two Philadelphia teenagers, fifteen-year-old Anthony Hogan and eighteen-year-old Marvin Bullock, shot Patrolman John McEntee in the back of the head as he sat in his patrol car, they said it was revenge for the police shooting a mentally disabled black man, Roger Allison, the week before.[26] In the aftermath of the Allison shooting, black activist Muhammed Kenyatta called a press conference at Panther headquarters, declaring, "Blacks die at the hands of police and it is called justifiable homicide. Police should die at the hands of the community and it should be called justifiable homicide."[27] Anger at police coursed through the city's black neighborhoods, and it did not take much to trigger a reaction. Murders, such as the killing of Officer McEntee, were committed by what Russell Shoats called "free shooters" (i.e., individuals who were politically motivated to attack police but who acted on their own rather than as part of a clandestine movement), and the growing number of these shootings fit the pattern of an increasingly hostile community facing off against the police force.[28]

Attacks on police—planned, unplanned, and opportunistic—occurred against a backdrop of excessive police violence that extended back decades in Philadelphia and in black communities across the country. Even when police violence was legally justifiable, the lack of investigations meant that doubts lingered and communities seethed as the number of such shootings accumulated.

The use of deadly force by police even today is difficult to research. There are few statistics on police shootings, and since most cases were handled in internal investigations closed to civilians and the press, there are few public records to draw upon.[29] Only the most egregious incidents left a trail, with outraged family and community members protesting the killing and the protests covered by the media. Yet these more public cases— presumably the least defensible of police shootings—confirm the consistent lack of police accountability that fed community resentment. Even when a police killing could not be considered legal by the standard of the day, internal police boards almost never disciplined an officer, district attorneys rarely indicted one, and juries even more rarely convicted an officer on those occasions when police were indicted.

The indictment of Officer Robert Marinelli in 1960 was therefore an unusual event, one that illuminates how difficult it was to hold police accountable for their actions. At first Marinelli was cleared of wrongdoing in a departmental investigation, with the district attorney concurring in the decision. Owing to tremendous community pressure, however, and a liberal mayoral administration supportive of civil rights, the police and the district attorney reversed their earlier decision and allowed a public accounting of the incident to go forward.

Marinelli had responded to a call about a shooting in North Philadelphia and, on arriving at the scene, saw a man running into an apartment. Without leaving his patrol car, Marinelli fired five shots, killing both the man, Emmanuel Thomas, and a bystander, Louise Jones, who was in the vestibule of the building into which Thomas had fled. But Thomas was the wrong man.

Thomas had been sitting on a doorstep with a friend when a fatally wounded man staggered downstairs and out into the street. The shooter, John Black, emerged from the house immediately thereafter, firing additional shots, and Thomas, fearful of being hit, ran and ducked for cover just as Officer Marinelli drove up. Meanwhile Louise Jones had gone to the door to see what the commotion was about, and a stray bullet hit her as

Thomas ran into the building. A ricocheted bullet grazed a passerby, while another ricochet narrowly missed hitting a sixteen-year-old boy returning from school, lodging in his books instead. Clearly a tragedy had occurred, and a worse one was narrowly avoided.

Marinelli's reckless shooting caused an uproar in the neighborhood and in the press. In addition to the victims, dozens of children had been playing on the street. Critics pointed out that a police officer would never have fired shots on a crowded street in a white neighborhood. The fact that Marinelli fired from within his car and without warning made his actions seem particularly egregious.

Mass rallies over the next few days put pressure on the district attorney's office to indict Patrolman Marinelli for homicide. Speakers, including the future judge A. Leon Higginbotham and Congressman Robert N. C. Nix, as well as ministers and community activists, were angry that Chief Inspector John Kelly had stated that Marinelli had acted "in good faith." After the district attorney cleared Marinelli of wrongdoing, black Philadelphians concluded that this was another official whitewash of a police shooting. Residents flooded the offices of Mayor Richardson Dilworth and District Attorney Victor Blanc with letters and phone calls, and about a hundred picketers showed up outside of City Hall on the day of Louise Jones's funeral, which attracted 4,500 mourners. In the face of public outrage and political pressure, District Attorney Blanc reversed course and indicted Marinelli.

Marinelli's attorneys delayed his trial for nearly a year, allowing public feelings to cool down and Marinelli's supporters to rally. When Marinelli was suspended for thirty days, the Fraternal Order of Police paid his salary and arranged for legal representation. After the suspension ended, Police Commissioner Thomas Gibbons reinstated him and assigned him to desk duty in City Hall. A thousand of Marinelli's neighbors rallied behind the beleaguered officer, and Councilman Thomas Foglietta called his indictment a "grave miscarriage of justice." As occurred frequently, opinions about the shooting split along racial lines.

Marinelli opted for a jury trial, and the defense issued preemptive challenges to all seven African American prospective jurors. The challenges left a jury that consisted of ten women and two men, all of whom were white, something Marinelli's attorney clearly hoped would make them more sympathetic to the officer. Marinelli's defense was simple: he observed someone running from the scene of a crime, and he was fearful because of the high crime rate in the neighborhood. When Thomas turned toward him and crouched, Marinelli fired in self-defense, fearing for his life. Police department supervisors supported his contention. Chief Inspector Kelly testified that he or any other officer would have done the same under similar circumstances. The jury agreed. After deliberating for a mere ninety-five minutes, it cleared Marinelli of all charges.[30]

While at minimum Marinelli showed a lack of good judgment in firing his weapon on a crowded street when no one was shooting at him, his actions were legal. Pennsylvania law at the time still followed common-law tradition and allowed a police officer to shoot a fleeing felon, especially one who was armed, and Marinelli had reason to believe that Thomas had just gunned someone down. Marinelli may have acted recklessly but without malice or premeditation. Just as district attorneys were reluctant to charge police officers, so too were juries—especially all-white juries—reluctant to convict officers making split-second decisions to shoot black suspects in ambiguous circumstances. This too was a pattern constantly repeated.

There were relatively few police killings of civilians in the 1950s and 1960s, but Frank Rizzo's tenure as police commissioner and then as mayor encouraged police officers to act more aggressively. As a larger-than-life individual, Rizzo personified the attitude and tough-guy character of the Philadelphia Police Department. There is no doubt that his swagger infused the department with a "we can do no wrong" attitude. Rizzo emboldened police with his attacks on African American activists and black and white radicals, and with his stalwart support of officers accused of physically abusing citizens. He employed the language of crime to appeal to white voters and posed the police as defenders of the "decent" people in the city.

When Rizzo moved to City Hall, he picked a longtime associate, Joseph F. O'Neill, as police commissioner. O'Neill not only ignored allegations of police abuse; he argued that any attempt to curb police aggressiveness would make the police force less effective and endanger the city. In response to criticism generated by hearings conducted by the United States Commission on Civil Rights in 1979, O'Neill retorted that investigations and the release of their findings would turn the police into "a bunch of pansies running around out there." At those hearings, Mayor Rizzo claimed that no pattern of police abuse existed. Rather, such claims were "media generated" by the *Inquirer* in order to sell papers.[31] The commission investigation arrived at different conclusions. It found that the department had a history of giving commendations to officers against whom complaints had been lodged, frequently for the same incident that had led to the complaint.[32] More disturbingly, department leadership also covered for officers involved in fatal shootings. O'Neill had suspended the department's "use of force" directive in 1973 just as Pennsylvania revised the common-law "fleeing felon" standard for justifiable homicide.[33] Thus, officers were left to their own discretion in deciding whether or not to use deadly force in a given situation, and with little guidance, it is not surprising that the number of shootings rose. O'Neill also shifted investigations of police homicides from Internal Affairs, where they were lodged in most major police forces, to the Homicide Squad, which itself would become the focus of allegations of misconduct, including extorted confessions and framed convictions, over the next several years.[34] Philadelphia police officers could fire their guns with impunity, knowing that few of their decisions would be seriously questioned.

At the same time, the 1970s saw more guns on the street and more people ready to use them. In my sample of homicide cases, the use of guns in murders doubled over time, from less than one-third in the 1940s and 1950s to about two-thirds in the late 1960s. Gun ownership increased over this period as well. In 1965 the city passed a handgun registration ordinance, and 3,540 people received permits to have a gun at home; in 1970 the number receiving permits increased to 8,240. Between 1965 and 1971, 38,802 people registered to buy handguns, significantly adding to the nearly 75,000 guns already registered under older legislation.[35] The number of unregistered guns in the city is unknowable, but the direction in gun ownership of all types was clear. More people were arming themselves—most likely in response to the escalating crime rate—and both registered and unregistered guns were stolen in burglaries or sold to new owners and made their way to the streets. Police aggressiveness and black resistance in a highly armed city primed the pump for lethal confrontations.

Winston Hood was not armed when he was shot by police, but as a Black Muslim, he was the sort of activist whose willingness to stand his ground in the face of police no doubt felt like a challenge to the officers who confronted him. The incident began at Foster's Lounge, a small bar at 23rd Street and Allegheny Avenue in North Philadelphia, where Hood and Thomas Nobblen were selling costume jewelry. Hood and Nobblen were dressed in the trademark garb of the Muslims—a black suit and white shirt with a black tie and black fez—and they made the rounds of North Philadelphia bars hawking their wares and preaching the teachings of the Nation of Islam. Hood and Nobblen were in Foster's when two men in the bar got into an argument, allegedly because one had insulted the barmaid. Hood and Nobblen intervened, and as the argument grew heated, the bartender ordered Nobblen and one of the men to go outside to settle the dispute. Hood and the other man, Daniel Younger, went outside as backup, but the argument fizzled and everyone had already made peace and shaken hands when Officer Henry Troutner pulled up after being alerted to a disturbance. Troutner saw that nothing was happening, but he ordered the two Muslims to halt as they were leaving the scene, demanding to see what was in the bag they were carrying. According to one witness, "The cop took one [Hood or Nobblen] by the arm, and the guy said to the cop, 'Hey, we can talk, but you don't have to grab me,'" and he pulled his arm away. By this time backup had arrived, and officers Rosemarie Trainor, Raymond Stratton, and George Michaels got into the argument with the two Muslims. "The Muslims kicked the lady cop. Then two other cops came and they started beating both of them up terrible," reported Helen Lyons, a neighbor.

At this point accounts begin to differ. According to police, Hood had grabbed Troutner's gun during the scuffle. Officer Stratton pulled his gun, and several of the other officers called on him to shoot, but he reholstered his weapon. Officer Peter Organsky, who had just arrived, jumped out of his car, and seeing Hood with a weapon, ordered him to drop it and then fired a shot into Hood's chest. According to police, Hood was handcuffed after he was shot and while he was on the ground.

Willma Mae Dendy recalled the scene somewhat differently. She saw Rosemarie Trainor fall and said that is when the other police began to beat the two men with their nightsticks. "I was still sitting in the car across the street, and they beat them to the ground." She and several other witnesses said that the two men had their hands behind their back, though they differed as to whether or not Hood and Nobblen were handcuffed. Dendy said that Hood was upright, with cuffs on, when Organsky arrived. "He got out of his car, walked over to Hood with his gun drawn and shot him. He walked right up to Hood and shot." Daniel Younger, who had been in the bar with Hood and Nobblen, recalled events similarly: "They had Winston and the other guy handcuffed behind their backs, and they were telling a black officer to shoot. The black officer hesitated . . . and a white officer ran around from his van and shot him from about five feet away in his chest." Melvina Spencer ran onto her porch thinking the bar was being robbed. She looked over and saw Hood on the ground, with his hands behind him, though she could not see whether he was cuffed. "I didn't see any handcuffs on him. But a cop was on his legs, holding him down and they was coming on him. One cop hollered, 'shoot!' and when the shot rang out, that boy was on the ground. They had him down with his hands behind his back before the shot was fired." Linwood Lyons, Helen's husband, reported that "the cop got out, and the guy lying on the ground originally started kicking, and the officer ran into one of his kicks. The officer fell back, pulled his pistol (and after walking part way around the man) went to one knee on the ground in front of the kicking man, took aim and shot him."[36] Witness accounts differed on several crucial details: some said Hood was on ground, with his hands behind him; others said he was upright when the shooting happened, which corresponded to the police account. Some said Organsky had been kicked and had staggered before firing, while others said he got out of his car, aimed at Hood, and shot. No one, except police, saw Hood with a gun, and neither did police supervisors arriving at the scene. After the shooting, Troutner claimed he had retrieved his weapon from the fallen Hood after Hood had wrested it from him.

The case against Officer Organsky came down to one of police credibility. A police department review and one by the district attorney's office cleared Organsky and the other officers of any wrongdoing, and no criminal charges were filed, although Hood's parents filed a wrongful death suit against the city and the police department. An investigation by the Justice Department found the eyewitness statements conflicting, concluding that some witnesses could not have seen what they claimed from the vantage points they had, and dropped its review of the case. Organsky applied for a disability pension for psychological reasons, and the city offered the Hood family a $100,000 settlement in their suit. Thomas Nobblen, who was severely beaten in the incident, went to trial for aggravated and simple assault against a police officer and resisting arrest. A jury took seventeen minutes to acquit him of the serious charges but found him guilty of disorderly conduct. Nobblen's attorney found that crucial police log books and incident reports were missing and suggested the strong possibility of a cover-up.[37]

In the nearly twenty years since the Marinelli shootings, very little had changed in the insular world of Philadelphia police. The parochial nature of the police, who tended to socialize with each other both because of the nature of the job and the shift work it entailed, the unavoidable reliance on individual discretion on the street, the need for absolute trust in one's partner in dangerous situations, the belief that some of the communities officers patrolled were both resentful and potentially dangerous, and the knowledge that there were many guns in citizens' hands all meant that police were extremely reluctant to second-guess the decisions of colleagues under conditions of extreme stress.[38] In fact, they were more likely to cover for one another, as in the Winston Hood case, than put an officer's career in jeopardy. Commanding officers were equally reluctant to challenge the decisions of the officers under their command. Investigators criticized the Philadelphia Police Department for blurring distinctions between management and rank and file, with commanders more likely to defend the interests of the rank and file than to investigate allegations against them.[39]

Political pressures external to the police department also had little effect on police practices. Despite investigations by the Department of Justice, hearings by the Civil Rights Commission, and lawsuits against the city, it remained nearly impossible to hold police accountable for their actions. Demonstrations at City Hall and protests before City Council had little impact in a city in which the Rizzo administration saw itself as the defender of the police and the police as the defenders of its white, ethnic constituents.

Yet, surprisingly, this seemingly intractable situation changed. During the 1980s, despite an increasing homicide rate, both police killings of civilians and intentional killings of police officers declined as the city stepped back from a violent abyss. The number of civilians killed by police in the city fell sharply, from an average of about eighteen per year in the 1970s to an average of seven per year in the 1980s, similar to the number in the 1960s. At the same time, the number of intentional killings of police fell to about half of what they had been the previous decade.

Nineteen Philadelphia police officers died during the 1980s, ten as a result of intentional killings.[40] How did things turn around so quickly?

When William Green became mayor in 1980, he entered City Hall with strong support from the city's African American community. Green's senior appointments signaled a changing of the guard in which blacks asserted new political power in City Hall. Green appointed Wilson Goode Philadelphia's first black managing director and Constance Clayton the first black superintendent of schools, while also supporting Joseph Coleman as the first black president of City Council.

His most significant appointment was a new police commissioner. Morton Solomon, was a twenty-nine-year veteran of the department, but he also was an outsider: the first Jewish police commissioner in a department dominated by Irish and Italian Catholics, and one dedicated to reform. Solomon instituted a community-education course at the Philadelphia Police Academy, appointed the department's first black deputy commissioner, and improved citizen-complaint procedures. Most importantly, in one of his first acts as commissioner, Solomon issued a use-of-force directive that strictly limited the instances in which police could fire their weapons, bringing them in accord with Pennsylvania law. A dramatic decline in police shootings followed.[41] Clearer guidelines, improved training, and new directions from the top in a hierarchical organization together made a difference in police use of force, especially since the political climate in the city had changed.[42] Just as Frank Rizzo's appointment as police commissioner and his election as mayor emboldened police to act more aggressively, with a consequent increase in police-initiated killings, the emergence of black political power and a reform administration cautioned police to act with more restraint.

The decline in police killings of civilians paralleled a decline in murders of Philadelphia police officers. Here both local and national trends were in play. Commissioner Solomon's efforts to improve community relations and to redefine the circumstances under which police could use lethal force clearly met the approval of the city's civil rights leaders and reduced the tensions between police and the black community. At the same time, the number of police officers killed in the United States peaked in the 1970s and fell steadily thereafter. In 1978, 1 policeman in 4,000 was murdered; in 1988, it was 1 in 6,000; and by 1998, that had fallen to 1 in 11,000 officers.

Perhaps the most important reason for the decline in police deaths was the routine use of body armor, which started in the 1970s. In Philadelphia, Morton Solomon raised the money needed to equip Philadelphia officers with bulletproof vests, just as police departments across the nation were doing. While police were still shot in the line of duty, body armor clearly increased the chances of surviving an attack.[43]

Just as importantly, the radical underground groups targeting police were virtually decimated by the end of the 1970s. The FBI's Operation COINTELPRO disrupted the Panthers' and other radical groups' ability to organize. The FBI spread misinformation about the Panthers, planted informants who sowed dissension within the ranks, and encouraged rivalry between black radical groups. Intense surveillance and routine harassment and arrests on minor charges kept members in a cycle of jail time and court appearances and sapped organizational energy and funds. Raids on Panther and other black revolutionary groups' headquarters in cities across the nation led to deadly shootouts and follow-up prosecutions resulting in lengthy prison sentences. FBI-promoted feuds with other black revolutionary groups led to several assassinations as the black underground splintered.[44]

Political power mattered here too, as cities in which black political power was evident showed fewer attacks on police.[45] In Philadelphia, Wilson Goode succeeded William Green in 1984 to become the city's first black mayor. While relations between the police and the black community remained troubled, and Goode's mayoralty was marred by the police department's bombing of the MOVE house in which eleven people, including five children, died, blacks had attained undeniable power in the city. The combination of suppression of radical groups and the incorporation of black political energies into electoral politics diffused the anger that had fueled the 1970s street wars.[46] The relative peace did not last. As young men turned to crime and drugs, and a new violent black underground emerged—a Black Mafia dedicated not to politics and revolution, but to power and greed—one era gave over to another. And yet, the crisis that marked the postwar transition persisted. As long as Philadelphia harbored an ecology of violence, murder in the city's black communities would continue to plague Philadelphia's reputation and the quality of its residents' lives.

# Notes

## Foreword

1. Marvin E. Wolfgang, *Patterns in Criminal Homicide* (Philadelphia: University of Pennsylvania Press, 1958), 330; Marvin E. Wolfgang and Franco Ferracuti, *The Subculture of Violence: Towards and Integrated Theory in Criminology* (London: Tavistock, 1967). Referencing the durability of the "criminal subculture that flourished in the later nineteenth century," Roger Lane concluded, "Many of the distinctive criminal patterns . . . are still evident late in the twentieth century." Lane, *Roots of Violence in Black Philadelphia, 1860–1900* (Cambridge, MA: Harvard University Press, 1986), 5.

2. Eric C. Schneider, *Smack: Heroin and the American City* (Philadelphia: University of Pennsylvania Press, 2008), 116–17. In dealing with the subject of crime in an entry for the *Encyclopedia of Greater Philadelphia*, Schneider reiterated his fundamental association of crime with poverty and place, writing in the opening sentence, "Crime is inextricably linked to Philadelphia's shifting economic fortunes." Schneider, "Crime," https://philadelphia encyclopedia.org/archive/crime/.

3. Robert J. Sampson and William Julius Wilson, "Toward a Theory of Race, Crime, and Urban Inequality," in *Crime and Inequality*, ed. John Hagan and Ruth D. Peterson (Stanford: Stanford University Press, 1995), 37–54.

4. Patrick Sharkey, Gerard Torrats-Espinosa, and Delaram Takyar, "Community and the Crime Decline: The Causal Effect of Local Nonprofits on Violent Crime," *American Sociological Review* 82 (December 2017): 1214–40; Patrick Sharkey, *Uneasy Peace: The Great Crime Decline, The Renewal of City Life, and the Next War on Violence* (New York: W. W. Norton, 2018); Emily Badger, "Ordinary Citizens' Unsung Role in the Crime Decline," *New York Times*, November 10, 2017.

5. Chris Palmer and Julia Terruso, "'I'm Very Lucky,' Oh Says as he Continues Healing at Home," *Philadelphia Inquirer*, June 2, 2017; Chris Palmer, "Spring Garden Man Shot Dead in Front of 2-year-old Daughter," *Philadelphia Inquirer*, September 8, 2017; and Julie Shaw, "1 of 2 Brothers in 2017 Slaying of Spring Garden Activist Gerard Grandzol Pleads Guilty to Murder," *Philadelphia Inquirer*, January 26, 2019.

6. Thomas P. Abt, "The Politics of Murder," *New York Times*, September 27, 2017. Abt's book, *Bleeding Out: The Devastating Consequences of Urban Violence—and a Bold New Plan for Peace in the Streets* (New York: Basic, 2019), offers a variation on Schneider's argument, that because violence is so closely related to urban poverty, curbing crime can unlock the untapped potential of the nation's most disadvantaged city communities.

7. Jill Leovy, *Ghettoside: A True Story of Murder in America* (New York: Spiegel & Grau, 2015), 9, 318–19.

8. Ira Lipman, "Introduction," in *Crime and Justice at the Millennium: Essays by and in Honor of Marvin E. Wolfgang*, ed. Robert A. Silverman, Terence P. Thornberry, Bernard Cohen, and Barry Krisberg (Boston: Kluwer, 2002), xi.

9. Guian A. McKee, *The Problem of Jobs: Liberalism Race, and Deindustrialization in Philadelphia* (Chicago: University of Chicago Press, 2008), 85; Schneider, "Crime"; David Elesh, "Deindustrialization," *Encyclopedia of Greater Philadelphia*, https://philadelphiaencyclopedia.org/archive/deindustrialization/.

10. John M. McLaron and G. Terry Madonna, "Dilworth, Clark, and Reform in Philadelphia, 1947–1962," *Legacies* 11 (November 2011): 25–31.

11. William Julius Wilson, *The Truly Disadvantaged: The Inner City, The Underclass and Public Policy* (Chicago: University of Chicago Press, 1987). Wilson's central contribution in addressing the changes that accompanied postwar disinvestment was to convey a new vision of communities and crime, one, as a resent assessment put it, "that attributed crime to truly disadvantaged structural circumstances rather than social disorganization." Paula Wilcox, Francis T. Cullen, and Ben Feldmeyder, *Communities and Crime: An Enduring American Challenge* (Philadelphia: Temple University Press, 2018), 60 and passim.

12. Matthew J. Countryman, *Up South: Civil Rights and Black Power in Philadelphia* (Philadelphia: University of Pennsylvania Press, 2006), 158–59.

13. Lenora E. Berson, *Case Study of a Riot: The Philadelphia Story* (New York: Institute of Human Relations Press, 1966), 27–28, 50. The last page of the AJC report featured an advertisement for Marvin Wolfgang's *Crime and Race*, and an associated reader's guide for discussion of the report further recommended the same volume.

14. Nancy Kleniewski, "Triage and Urban Planning: A Case Study of Philadelphia," *International Journal of Urban and Regional Research* 10 (December 1986): 571–72.

15. Nutter's story appeared as part of an account of widescale kickbacks to a handful of police operating in North Philadelphia. Debbie Goldberg, "For Many in North Philadelphia, Police Corruption Is No Surprise," *Philadelphia Inquirer*, October 5, 1995.

16. St. Clair Drake and Horace R. Cayton, *Black Metropolis: A Study of Negro Life in a Northern City* (Chicago: University of Chicago Press, 2015 ed.), chap. 17, "Business Under a Cloud;" Pennsylvania Crime Commission, *Report on Police Corruption and the Quality of Law Enforcement in Philadelphia*, March, 1974, 1.

17. Khalil Gibran Muhammad, *The Condemnation of Blackness: Race Crime, and the Making of Modern Urban America* (Cambridge, MA: Harvard University Press, 2010). Although Muhammad's argument is broad, he focuses his assessment of the racialization of crime statistics and their effects on the half-century of Philadelphia experience before World War II.

18. As part of the settlement of the 2010 *Bailey et al. v. City of Philadelphia* court case that demonstrated the disparate treatment of African Americans stopped under "reasonable suspicion" to be frisked, the ACLU of Pennsylvania has recorded rates that continue to show that black pedestrians are 75 percent more likely to be frisked than white detainees. See ACLU Pennsylvania, "Bailey, et al. v. City of Philadelphia, et al.," https://www.aclupa.org/our-work/legal/legaldocket/baileyetalvcityofphiladelp. Historically, Philadelphia ranked high among major cities in a follow-up study to the 1968 Kerner Commission report on civil disorders, in

both the practice of frisking black men and search executed without warrant. Peter H. Rossi, Richard A. Berk, and Bettye E. Eidson, *The Roots of Urban Discontent: Public Policy, Municipal Institutions and the Ghetto* (New York: Wiley: 1974), 137. Significantly, Rossi and his colleagues, on page 203, conclude a summary of their assessment of metropolitan police by asserting, "They tend to form an occupational community, and in relation to the black communities in which they patrol perceived themselves in many cities as almost an occupying force in a hostile and uncooperative environment."

19. From highs of 44.3 homicides per 100,000 persons in 1985 and 1988, murder rates fell with those across the country's major cities to a low of 15.9 in 2013 and 2014, when the rate rose again to 22.2 in 2018. In each year of the compilation, Philadelphia's murder rate was approximately four times that of the country as a whole. While a map depicting homicides for 2017 showed a good number on the city's west side, the greatest number concentrated in eight of the nine wards north of downtown. Chris Palmer, "Deadliest Year Since 2012 at 300-plus," *Philadelphia Inquirer*, January 1, 2018.

## Preface

1. "Blacks have been considerably more likely than whites to be killed by murders in the US for as long as good records have been available," according to the O'Flaherty and Sethi report. Aggregate rates of homicide and victimization depend, they conclude, "on the frequency with which members of different groups come into contact with each other. This depends on the level of segregation in social interactions, as well as the demographic composition of the population at large." Brendan O'Flaherty and Rajiv Sethi, "Homicide in Black and White," *Journal of Urban Economics* 68 (November 2010): 217, 216.

## Chapter 1

1. Darnell F. Hawkins, "Black and White Homicide Differentials: Alternatives to an Inadequate Theory," in *Homicide Among Black Americans*, ed. Darnell F. Hawkins (Lanham, MD: University Press of America, 1986), 109–35; Reynolds Farley, "Homicide Trends in the United States," in Hawkins, *Homicide Among Black Americans*, 13–27; Harold M. Rose, "Lethal Aspects of Urban Violence: An Overview," in *Lethal Aspects of Urban Violence*, ed. Harold M. Rose (Lexington, MA: Lexington Books, 1979), 1–16; Youngsock Sin, Davor Jedlicka, and Everett S. Lee, "Homicide Among Blacks," *Phylon* 38, no. 4 (1977): 398–407.

2. In Cleveland, for example, the three "planning areas" with the highest concentration of African Americans also accounted for 6 percent of the city's homicides. See Robert C. Bensing and Oliver Schroeder Jr., *Homicide in an Urban Community* (Springfield, IL: C. C. Thomas, 1960); Harold M. Rose, "The Geography of Despair," *Annals of the American Association of Geographers* 68 (December 1978): 453–64; Richard Block, "Homicide in Chicago: A Nine-Year Study (1965–1973)," *Journal of Criminal Law and Criminology* 66 (December 1975): 496–510. See Marvin Wolfgang's *Patterns in Criminal Homicide* (Philadelphia: University of Pennsylvania Press, 1958); Wolfgang found that 19 percent of homicides from 1948 to 1952 occurred in census tracts containing 3 percent of the city's population. For the nineteenth century, see Roger Lane, *The Roots of Violence in Black Philadelphia, 1860–1900* (Cambridge, MA: Harvard University Press, 1986); and Jeffrey Adler, "Murder, North and South: Violence in Early-Twentieth-Century Chicago and New Orleans," *Journal of Southern History* 74 (May 2008): 297–324.

3. See Figure 1, based on data from the Philadelphia Department of Public Health annual reports, Philadelphia City Archives.

4. For a critique of progressive intellectuals' tendency to downplay or ignore negative characteristics of inner-city communities, see Loic Wacquant, "Scrutinizing the Street: Poverty, Morality, and the Pitfalls of Urban Ethnography," *American Journal of Sociology* 107 (May 2002): 1468–532; and Philippe Bourgois, *In Search of Respect: Selling Crack in El Barrio* (New York: Cambridge University Press, 1996).

5. Fox Butterfield, *All God's Children: The Bosket Family and the American Tradition of Violence* (New York: Avon, 1996); Ruth E. Dennis, "The Role of Homicide in Decreasing Life Expectancy," in Rose, *Lethal Aspects of Urban Violence*, 17–30; Thomas F. Pettigrew and Rosalind Barclay Spier, "The Ecological Structure of Negro Homicide," *American Journal of Sociology* 67 (May 1962): 621–29.

6. Sheldon Hackney, "Southern Violence," in *Violence in America: A Report to the National Commission on the Causes and Prevention of Violence*, ed. Hugh Davis Graham and Ted Robert Gurr (New York: Bantam, 1969), 505–27; Raymond D. Gastil, "Homicide and a Regional Culture of Violence," *American Sociological Review* 36 (June 1971): 412–27.

7. Colin Loftin and Robert H. Hill, "Regional Subculture and Homicide: An Examination of the Gastil-Hackney Thesis," *American Sociological Review* 39 (October 1974): 714–24; Howard Erlanger, "Is There a 'Subculture of Violence' in the South?" *Journal of Criminal Law and Criminology* 66 (December 1975): 483–90.

8. Marvin E. Wolfgang and Franco Ferracuti, *The Subculture of Violence: Towards an Integrated Theory in Criminology* (London: Tavistock, 1967), esp. 152–56. Wolfgang's belief that criminal homicide emanated from a subculture of violence emerged as early as his 1958 study of Philadelphia. See Wolfgang, *Patterns in Criminal Homicide*, 329. Their theory that a distinct value system "provides its members with normative support for their violent behavior" is thoroughly challenged by Liqun Cao, Anthony Troy Adams, and Vickie J. Jensen, in "The Empirical Status of the Black-Subculture-of-Violence Thesis," in *The System in Black and White: Exploring the Connections Between Race, Crime, and Justice*, ed. Michael W. Markowitz and Delores D. Jones-Brown (Westport, CT: Praeger, 2000), 47–61. After running a series of correlations to test Wolfgang and Ferracuti's contentions, the authors conclude, "Based on our data and analyses, there is enough evidence to conclude that blacks in the general population are no more likely than whites to embrace values favorable to violence" (58).

9. Robert J. Sampson and Lydia Bean, "Cultural Mechanisms and Killing Fields: A Revised Theory of Community-Level Racial Inequality," in *The Many Colors of Crime*, ed. Ruth D. Peterson, Lauren J. Krivo, and John Hagan (New York: New York University Press, 2006), 8–36.

10. Elijah Anderson, "The Social Ecology of Youth Violence, "*Crime and Justice* 24 (1998): 65–104; Elijah Anderson, *Code of the Street: Decency, Violence, and the Moral Life of the Inner City* (New York: W. W. Norton, 1999).

11. Bourgois, *In Search of Respect*.

12. Martin Daly and Margo Wilson, *Homicide* (New Brunswick, NJ: Transaction, 1988).

13. David T. Courtwright, *Violent Land: Single Men and Social Disorder from the Frontier to the Inner City* (Cambridge, MA: Harvard University Press, 1996).

14. See Adler, "Murder, North and South."

15. Norbert Elias, *The Civilizing Process*, trans. Edmund Jephcott (Cambridge, MA: Blackwell, 1994); Pieter Spierenburg, *A History of Murder: Personal Violence in Europe from the Middle Ages to the Present* (Cambridge: Polity, 2008); Stephen Mennell, *The American Civilizing Process* (Cambridge: Polity, 2007); Jeffrey S. Adler, *First in Violence, Deepest in Dirt: Homicide in Chicago, 1875–1920* (Cambridge, MA: Harvard University Press, 2006).

16. Pieter Spierenburg, "Democracy Came Too Early: A Tentative Explanation for the Problem of American Homicide," *American Historical Review* 111 (February 2006): 104–14.

17. Randolph Roth, "American Homicide Supplemental Volume: Civilization Thesis," Historical Violence Database, http://cjrc.osu.edu/researchprojects/hvd/AHsup.html, accessed February 19, 2010.

18. Manuel Eisner, "Long-Term Historical Trends in Violent Crime," *Crime and Justice: A Review of Research* 30 (2003): 83–142.

19. Loic Wacquant, "Decivilizing and Demonizing: The Remaking of the Black American Ghetto," in *The Sociology of Norbert Elias*, ed. Steven Loyal and Stephen Quilley (Cambridge: Cambridge University Press, 2004), 95–121.

20. Lane, *Roots of Violence*, passim; Roger Lane, *Murder in America: A History* (Columbus: Ohio State University Press, 1997).

21. Randolph Roth, *American Homicide* (Cambridge, MA: Harvard University Press, 2009), 391.

22. Gary LaFree, *Losing Legitimacy: Street Crime and the Decline of Social Institutions in America* (Boulder, CO: Westview, 1998).

23. Roth, *American Homicide*, chap. 9.

24. Douglas S. Massey, Gretchen A. Condran, and Nancy Denton, "The Effect of Residential Segregation on Black Economic and Social Well-Being," *Social Forces* 66 (September 1987): 29–56; Douglas S. Massey and Nancy Denton, *American Apartheid: Segregation and the Making of the Underclass* (Cambridge, MA: Harvard University Press, 1993); Edward S. Shihadeh and Nicole Flynn, "Segregation and Crime: The Effect of Black Social Isolation on the Rates of Black Urban Violence," *Social Forces* 74 (June 1996): 1325–352; William Julius Wilson, *The Declining Significance of Race: Blacks and Changing American Institutions* (Chicago: University of Chicago Press, 1980); Robert J. Sampson and William Julius Wilson, "Toward a Theory of Race, Crime, and Urban Inequality," in *Crime and Inequality*, ed. John Hagan and Ruth D. Peterson (Stanford: Stanford University Press, 1995), 37–54; Matthew R. Lee, "Concentrated Poverty, Race and Homicide," *Sociological Quarterly* 41 (Spring 2000): 189–206, shows how the Massey and Wilson hypotheses are complementary.

25. G. Gordon Brown, *Law Administration and Negro-White Relations in Philadelphia: A Study in Race Relations* (Philadelphia: Bureau of Municipal Research of Philadelphia, 1947), 44, 48, 115; Matthew J. Countryman: *Up South: Civil Rights and Black Power in Philadelphia* (Philadelphia: University of Pennsylvania Press, 2006), 49–53.

26. Eric C. Schneider, *Vampires, Dragons and Egyptian Kings: Youth Gangs in Postwar New York* (Princeton: Princeton University Press, 1999).

27. Notably, while Brown found that African American migrants from the South, who constituted more than 60 percent of the city's black population, brought with them a distrust of law enforcement, that bias was widely shared with established residents. Moreover, he reported, there was no evidence that children of migrant families contributed more to delinquency than those of nonmigrant families. *Law Administration and Negro-White Relations*,

30, 102–3, 78. The Kerner Commission confirmed Brown's judgment, singling out Philadelphia and San Diego as cities where African Americans "are convinced that the police apply a different standard of law enforcement in the ghettos." *Report of the National Advisory Commission on Civil Disorders* (New York: Bantam, 1968), 308. In his assessment of the research he did on behalf of the Kerner Commission, Johns Hopkins University sociologist Peter Rossi, after assessing police-community relations in thirteen cities, including Philadelphia, concluded that "ghetto policemen are hardly sympathetic to blacks and, to the contrary, often see the population of the ghetto as hostile and unfriendly." Peter H. Rossi, Richard A. Berk, and Bettye K. Eidson, *The Roots of Urban Discontent: Public Policy, Municipal Institutions, and the Ghetto* (New York: Wiley, 1974), 116.

28. James Wolfinger, "The Limits of Black Activism: Philadelphia's Public Housing in the Depression and World War II," *Journal of Urban History* 35 (September 2009): 787–814; John Bauman, *Public Housing, Race, and Renewal: Urban Planning in Philadelphia, 1920–1974* (Philadelphia: Temple University Press, 1987), chap. 8; John T. McGreevy, *Parish Boundaries: The Catholic Encounter with Race in the Twentieth-Century Urban North* (Chicago: University of Chicago Press, 1996).

29. Wilson, *Declining Significance of Race*; Sampson and Wilson, "Toward a Theory of Race, Crime, and Urban Inequality"; Sampson and Bean, "Cultural Mechanisms and Killing Fields."

30. Pierre Bourdieu and Loic Wacquant, "Symbolic Violence," in *Violence in Peace and War*, ed. Nancy Scheper-Hughes and Philippe Bourgois (Malden, MA: Blackwell, 2004), 272–74; Pierre Bourdieu, "Social Space and Symbolic Power," *Sociological Theory* 7 (June 1989): 18–26; George Karandinos, "'You Ridin'? The Moral Economy of Violence in North Philadelphia," Senior Honors Thesis for Health and Societies, University of Pennsylvania, Fall 2009.

31. I used a selective sample and picked every fourth case involving charges of first- or second-degree murder or voluntary manslaughter. The statistics in the text are for all cases, not just those involving African Americans, unless otherwise specified. All information is from Notes of Testimony, Philadelphia Court of Quarter Sessions, Philadelphia City Archives. Conclusions about homicide generally have to be tempered by the fact that only about 60 percent of the homicides in the city were prosecuted in court. The "gold standard" of criminologists is the police homicide investigation, where approximately 90 percent of the cases are cleared. However, the loss of statistical validity is offset by the wealth of qualitative information contained in the trial record.

32. Wolfgang's more complete analysis of homicide in Philadelphia between 1948 and 1952, based on police investigations, found that 73 percent of the victims and 75 percent of the alleged perpetrators were African American. *Patterns in Criminal Homicide*, 31.

33. These categories are roughly similar to Wolfgang's; I collapsed paramour or mistress homicides into my family/relationship ones and acquaintances and friends into a single group, and instead of "stranger" I used "dispute" to account for homicides between strangers. See Wolfgang, *Patterns in Criminal Homicide*, 207.

34. For a restatement of classical criminology, see Michael R. Gottfredson and Travis Hirschi, *A General Theory of Crime* (Stanford: Stanford University Press, 1990).

35. *Commonwealth vs. John Byrd*, March Sessions, 1943. Wolfgang found alcohol present as part of the "homicide situation" in nearly two-thirds of all killings. *Patterns in Criminal Homicide*, 136.

36. Adler found that drunken brawls fell from first to eighth place in the causes of homicide in Chicago between 1880 and 1920, arguing that industrial work and commercial leisure "civilized" plebeian working-class culture. *First in Violence, Deepest in Dirt*, 40–43.

37. *Commonwealth v. Ernest Jordan*, April Sessions, 1946.

38. Wolfgang, *Patterns in Criminal Homicide*, 207.

39. *Commonwealth v. Frank Newton*, September Sessions, 1949.

40. *Commonwealth v. Archie Burney*, April Sessions, 1942,

41. *Commonwealth v. Joseph Harvey*, June Sessions, 1949; for a similar case, *Commonwealth v. Hines*, October Sessions, 1942.

42. See Lawrence W. Levine, *Black Culture and Black Consciousness: Afro-American Folk Thought from Slavery to Freedom* (New York: Oxford University Press, 1977), 407–20.

43. Wolfgang, *Patterns in Criminal Homicide*, 84.

44. *Commonwealth v. James Jackson*, April Sessions, 1947.

45. Leroy G. Schultz, a probation and parole officer for the Circuit Court for Criminal Causes in St. Louis, writing in 1962, documented a similar situation in St. Louis's inner-city areas. The largest number of offenders in his sample said they carried weapons because they were anticipating attack. His respondents, feeling that "protection available through police and courts was inadequate," Schultz reported, felt they must protect themselves and settle their own disputes. The group's attitudes could be summed up, he contended, in the words of one offender, who asserted, "I'd rather be caught by an officer with a weapon than to ever be caught by some of the folks on my street, without it." Although those in Schultz's sample were overwhelmingly recent migrants from the South in contrast to those convicted of crimes in Philadelphia, that could well have been a factor of St. Louis's location as a gateway from the South.

46. *Commonwealth v. Oliver Euell*, October Sessions, 1941.

47. *Commonwealth v. Arthur Wilson*, October Sessions, 1945.

48. *Commonwealth v. Hilbert Johnson*, January Sessions, 1947.

49. *Commonwealth v. Andrew Vance*, August Sessions, 1941.

50. *Commonwealth v. Charlotte Anderson*, July Sessions, 1949.

51. *Commonwealth v. Peggy Lloyd*, December Sessions, 1947.

52. *Commonwealth v. Erseline Carter*, February Sessions, 1945.

53. *Commonwealth v. Sadie Washington and Charles Armstead*, March Sessions, 1947.

54. Franklin E. Zimring, Joel Eigen, and Sheila O'Malley distinguish between what they call "wholesale" and "retail" homicides, with those crossing racial lines, including the felony homicides, in the latter category. "Homicide in Philadelphia: Perspectives on the Death Penalty," *University of Chicago Law Review* 43 (Winter 1976): 227–52.

55. In the pre-Miranda era, attorneys were generally not present, and defendants were warned that their statements could be used against them only at the point when a confession was about to be dictated—that is, after it had already been given orally.

56. *Commonwealth v. Theodore Elliott*, February Sessions, 1950.

57. Allan M. Winkler, "The Philadelphia Transit Strike of 1944," *Journal of American History* 59 (June 1972): 73–89; James Wolfinger, *Running the Rails: Capital and Labor in the Philadelphia Transit Industry* (Ithaca, NY: Cornell University Press, 2016), 122–59.

58. *Commonwealth v. John Scott*, June Sessions, 1946.

59. *Commonwealth v. Herbert Harris*, May Sessions, 1944.

60. *Commonwealth v. George Norris*, March Sessions, 1944.

61. Such calculations were widely perceived in the black community itself when criminal incidents involved black offenses against other African Americans, according to G. Gordon Brown's 1947 survey for the Bureau of Municipal Research of Philadelphia: *Law Administration and Negro-White Relations in Philadelphia*, 104.

62. Wolfinger, "Limits of Black Activism."

63. Countryman, *Up South*.

## Chapter 2

1. Marvin Wolfgang, *Patterns in Criminal Homicide* (Philadelphia: University of Pennsylvania Press, 1958); Harold M. Rose and Paula D. McClain, *Race, Place and Risk: Black Homicide in Urban America* (Albany: State University of New York Press, 1990); Jeffrey S. Adler, "'Bessie Done Cut Her Old Man': Race, Common-Law Marriage, and Homicide in New Orleans, 1925–1945," *Journal of Social History* 44 (Fall 2010): 123–43.

2. Margo I. Wilson and Martin Daly, "Who Kills Whom in Spouse Killings? On the Exceptional Sex Ratio of Spousal Homicide in the United States," *Criminology* 30 (November 1992): 189–215.

3. Joseph D. Lohman and Gordon Misner, President's Commission on Law Enforcement and Administration of Justice, *The Police and the Community: The Dynamics of Their Relationship in a Changing Society* (Washington, DC, 1966), vol. 2.

4. *Commonwealth v. John Byrd*, March Sessions, 1943; Leroy G. Schultz, "Why the Negro Carries Weapons," *Journal of Criminal Law, Criminology and Police Science* 53 (December 1962): 476–83.

5. I am indebted here to Bourdieu's concept of "habitus." See Pierre Bourdieu, "Social Space and Symbolic Power," *Sociological Theory* 7 (June 1989): 18–26.

6. Jacquelyn C. Campbell, "'If I Can't Have You, No One Can': Power and Control in Homicide of Female Partners," in *Femicide: The Politics of Woman Killing*, ed. Jill Radford and Diana E. H. Russell (New York: Twayne, 1992), 99–113; R. Emerson Dobash and Russell P. Dobash, "What Were They Thinking? Men Who Murdered an Intimate Partner," *Violence Against Women* 17 (January 2011): 111–34; Charles Patrick Ewing, *Fatal Families: The Dynamics of Intrafamilial Homicide* (Thousand Oaks, CA: Sage, 1997), chap. 2.

7. Wolfgang, *Patterns in Criminal Homicide*, chap. 14.

8. Roger Lane, *Murder in America: A History* (Columbus: Ohio State University Press, 1997), chap. 6.

9. Jeffrey S. Adler found a different pattern in Chicago, where the domestic homicide rate tracked increases in homicide more generally. "'We've Got a Right to Fight; We're Married': Domestic Homicide in Chicago, 1875–1920," *Journal of Interdisciplinary History* 36 (Summer 2003): 27–48.

10. *Commonwealth v. Grover Richards*, March Sessions, 1946; *Commonwealth v. Howard Brock*, October Sessions, 1946.

11. Roger Lane, *Roots of Violence in Black Philadelphia, 1860–1900* (Cambridge, MA: Harvard University Press, 1986); Lane, *Violent Death in the City: Suicide, Accident, and Murder in Nineteenth-Century Philadelphia* (Columbus: Ohio State University Press, 1999), 102–12; Wolfgang, *Patterns in Criminal Homicide*, 38.

12. Dobash and Dobash, "What Were They Thinking?"; R. P. Dobash and R. E. Dobash, "The Myth of Sexual Symmetry in Marital Violence," *Social Problems* 39 (February 1992);

Kenneth Polk, *When Men Kill: Scenarios of Masculine Violence* (Cambridge: Cambridge University Press, 1994), chap. 3. The classic pattern of stalking followed by a murder-suicide was comparatively rare.

13. Dane Archer and Rosemary Gartner, *Violence and Crime in Cross-National Perspective* (New Haven: Yale University Press, 1984).

14. Charles Patrick Ewing, *Battered Women Who Kill: Psychological Self-Defense as Legal Justification* (Lexington, MA: Lexington Books, 1987).

15. *Commonwealth v. Evelyn Newman*, January Sessions, 1960.

16. Wolfgang, *Patterns in Criminal Homicide*, 38; Adler, "Bessie Done Cut Her Old Man"; Jeffrey S. Adler, "Murder, North and South: Violence in Early-Twentieth-Century Chicago and New Orleans," *Journal of Southern History* 74 (May 2008): 297–324. On continuing high levels of intimate partner homicide among African Americans, see Victoria Fry, Vanessa Hosein, Eve Waltermaurer, Shannon Blaney, and Susan Wilt, "Femicide in New York City, 1990–1999," *Homicide Studies* 9 (August 2005): 204–28; Carolyn Rebecca Block and Antigone Christakos, "Intimate Partner Homicide in Chicago over 29 Years," *Crime and Delinquency* 41 (October 1995): 496–526; Eduardo Azziz-Baumgartner, Loreta McKeown, Patrice Melvin, Quynh Dang, and Joan Reed, "Rates of Femicide in Women of Different Races, Ethnicities, and Places of Birth: Massachusetts, 1993–2007," *Journal of Interpersonal Violence* 26 (March 2011): 1077–90; Wilson and Daly, "Who Kills Whom?"

17. Matthew J. Countryman, *Up South: Civil Rights and Black Power in Philadelphia* (Philadelphia: University of Pennsylvania Press, 2006), chaps. 1 and 2; G. Gordon Brown, *Law Administration and Negro-White Relations in Philadelphia: A Study in Race Relations* (Philadelphia: Bureau of Municipal Research of Philadelphia, 1947), 102–3; Lane, *Murder in America*, 350–51.

18. Wolfgang, *Patterns in Criminal Homicide*, 129.

19. *Commonwealth v. Charles Speller*, March Sessions, 1954.

20. *Commonwealth v. Leroy Turner*, May Sessions, 1954.

21. Delores P. Aldridge, "African-American Women in the Economic Marketplace: A Continuing Struggle," *Journal of Black Studies* 20 (December 1989): 129–54; Adler, "Bessie Done Cut Her Old Man." In their classic study of Chicago's South Side in the 1930s, St. Clair Drake and Horace R. Cayton depicted what they described as the lower-class black woman's superior economic position and how that influenced her view of an acceptable mate who, because of the vicissitudes of employment, might not be able to contribute much economically to a relationship: "A 'good old man' may perhaps slap or curse his 'old woman' if he's angry; he definitely will not 'beat her all the time' when he's sober, and will not endanger her life when drunk." *Black Metropolis: A Study of Negro Life in a Northern City* (Chicago: University of Chicago Press, 2015), 586–87.

22. *Commonwealth v. Margaret Jeffrey*, February Sessions, 1952.

23. *Commonwealth v. Loila Alicia Fuller*, July Sessions, 1956.

24. *Commonwealth v. John Snipes*, March Sessions, 1956.

25. Adler, "Bessie Done Cut Her Old Man"; Dobash et al., "Not an Ordinary Guy." Noel A. Cazenave and Margaret Zahn find that homicide is positively associated with non–state sanctioned relationships. I found no difference between married and nonmarried couples in my survey. Cazenave and Zahn, "Women, Murder and Male Domination: Police Reports of Domestic Violence in Chicago and Philadelphia," in *Intimate Violence: Interdisciplinary Perspectives*, ed. Emilio C. Viano (Washington, DC: Hemisphere, 1992), 83–97.

26. *Commonwealth v. Stanley Johnson,* January Sessions, 1957.

27. *Commonwealth v. Edward Riley,* October Sessions, 1957.

28. *Commonwealth v. Ella Louise Allen,* June Sessions, 1943. On the lack of police response, see Angela Browne, Kirk R. Williams, and Donald G. Dutton, "Homicide Between Intimate Partners: A 20-Year Review," in *Homicide: A Sourcebook of Social Research,* ed. M. Dwayne Smith and Margaret Zahn (Thousand Oaks, CA: Sage, 1999): 149–64; Doris Del Tosto, "The Battered Spouse Syndrome as a Defense to a Homicide Charge Under the Pennsylvania Criminal Code," *Villanova Law Review* 26 (1981): 105–34; Ewing, *Fatal Families,* chap. 2; Police Foundation, *Domestic Violence and the Police: Studies in Detroit and Kansas City* (n.p., 1977); Vickie Jensen, *Why Women Kill: Homicide and Gender Equality* (Boulder, CO: Lynne Rienner, 2001), 49.

29. *Commonwealth v. Ola Wilson,* October Sessions, 1945.

30. Wilson and Daly, "Who Kills Whom?"

31. *Commonwealth v. Nellie Hatch,* August Sessions, 1950.

32. *Commonwealth v. Charlotte Anderson,* July Sessions, 1949.

33. Ewing, *Battered Women Who Kill* and *Fatal Families;* Cynthia K. Gillespie, *Justifiable Homicide: Battered Women, Self-Defense, and the Law* (Columbus: Ohio State University Press, 1989).

## Chapter 3

1. Harley Etienne, *Pushing Back the Gates: Neighborhood Perspectives on University-Driven Revitalization in West Philadelphia* (Philadelphia: Temple University Press, 2012); "Last Store Standing: The Past and Present of McDonald's at 40th and Walnut," *Daily Pennsylvanian,* April 11, 2011. Etienne noted that each informant that he interviewed who had been associated with Penn for more than five years "had a crime-related horror story of some kind" (p. 37).

2. John L. Puckett and Mark Frazier Lloyd, "Martin Meyerson's Dream of 'One University': The Penn Presidency 1970–81 and Beyond," *Journal of Planning History* 10 (August 2011): 193–218; John L. Puckett and Mark Frazier Lloyd, *Becoming Penn: The Pragmatic American University, 1950–2000* (Philadelphia: University of Pennsylvania Press, 2015).

3. Arnold R. Hirsch, *Making the Second Ghetto: Race and Housing in Chicago, 1940–1960* (Cambridge: Cambridge University Press, 1983), chap. 5; Margaret Pugh O'Mara, *Cities of Knowledge: Cold War Science and the Search for the Next Silicon Valley* (Princeton: Princeton University Press, 2005); Michael Carriere, "Fighting the War Against Blight: Columbia University, Morningside Heights, Inc., and Counterinsurgent Urban Renewal," *Journal of Planning History* 10 (February 2011): 5–29; J. Mark Souther, "Acropolis of the Middle-West: Decay, Renewal, and Boosterism in Cleveland's University Circle," *Journal of Planning History* 10 (February 2011): 30–58; LaDale Winling, "Students and the Second Ghetto: Federal Legislation, Urban Politics, and Campus Planning at the University of Chicago," *Journal of Planning History* 10 (February 2011): 59–86.

4. Exceptions include Souther, "Acropolis of the Middle-West"; Puckett and Lloyd, "Martin Meyerson's Dream"; Howard Gillette Jr., *Camden After the Fall: Decline and Renewal in a Post-Industrial City* (Philadelphia: University of Pennsylvania Press, 2005); and Alan Ehrenhalt, *Lost City: Discovering the Forgotten Virtues of Community in the Chicago of the 1950s* (New York: Basic, 1995).

5. Elyse Sudow, "Displacement Demonized?: Towards an Alternative Explanation for Penn's Poor Relationship with West Philadelphia," history honors thesis, University of Pennsylvania, 1999, 42–43; G. Gordon Brown, *Law Administration and Negro-White Relations in Philadelphia: A Study in Race Relations* (Philadelphia: Bureau of Municipal Research of Philadelphia, 1947).

6. All quotations are from *Commonwealth v. Alfonso Borum*, May Sessions 1958, September 26, 1958, Notes of Testimony, Court of Quarter Sessions, Department of Records, City of Philadelphia.

7. "Phila. Mayor Weeps at Rite for Victim of Young Gang," *New York Herald Tribune*, April 30, 1958; "Murder: Stranger from Afar," *Newsweek*, May 12, 1958; "Gang Murders Korean Student in West Phila.," *Philadelphia Evening Bulletin*, April 26, 1958. These and subsequent clippings except for those from the *Philadelphia Tribune* can be found in folder In-Ho Oh, Alumni Records Collection, University of Pennsylvania Archives (UPA). The Temple Urban Archives (TUA) holds the morgue of the *Philadelphia Evening Bulletin*.

8. Statement of Mr. X [Joseph Williams], *Commonwealth v. Borum*.

9. "4th Defendant Gets Life Term in Murder of In-Ho Oh," *Philadelphia Evening Bulletin*, April 8, 1959.

10. *Commonwealth v. James Wright*, May Sessions 1958, April 6, 1960.

11. "Life Term Is Given Scoleri by 2–1 Ruling," *Philadelphia Inquirer*, February 27, 1959.

12. "Pal Sticks to Story Borum Kicked Oh," *Philadelphia Daily News*, October 1, 1958.

13. Statement of Joseph Williams, *Commonwealth v. Borum*.

14. "Bail Denied 11 in 'Jungle' Slaying; Blanc Asks Adult Trial, Death for All," *Philadelphia Evening Bulletin*, April 30, 1958.

15. This is based on my 20 percent sample of homicide trial transcripts from the Court of Quarter Sessions.

16. See Eric C. Schneider, *Vampires, Dragons and Egyptian Kings: Youth Gangs in Postwar New York* (Princeton: Princeton University Press, 1999); "Take Away Their Deadly Weapons," editorial, *Philadelphia Inquirer*, May 2, 1958; "Gang Murders Korean Student in West Phila.," *Philadelphia Evening Bulletin*, April 26, 1958; "Challenge," editorial, *Philadelphia Daily News*, April 29, 1958; "Wipe Out the Savage Street Gangs," editorial, *Philadelphia Inquirer*, September 1, 1959.

17. "Wipe Out Savage Street Gangs," editorial, *Philadelphia Inquirer*, April 29, 1958; "Crime, No Punishment," editorial, *Philadelphia Evening Bulletin*, October 22, 1958. There were two separate editorials with the same title about savage gangs.

18. "11 Lashed as 'Vermin' and Held Without Bail in Killing of Student," *Philadelphia Inquirer*, May 1, 1958; "Teen Slayers Riot in Cell at City Hall," *Philadelphia Inquirer*, June 24, 1958; Schneider, *Vampires*, introduction. According to the *Philadelphia Tribune*, no "riot" took place in the jail. See "In-Ho Oh's Killers Trial Postponed to Sept. 15th; In-Ho Oh Killers Didn't Riot," *Philadelphia Tribune*, July 1, 1958.

19. "9 Boys Seized in Murder of Penn Student," *Philadelphia Evening Bulletin*, April 27, 1958; "11 Boys Now Under Arrest in Slaying of Penn Student," *Philadelphia Evening Bulletin*, April 28, 1958; "Killing Called 'Jungle-Like,' 11 Denied Bail," *Philadelphia Evening Bulletin*, April 30, 1958.

20. "11 Lashed as 'Vermin' and Held without Bail in Killing of Student," *Philadelphia Inquirer*, May 1, 1958; "Why They Don't Cringe," editorial, *Philadelphia Evening Bulletin*, May 2, 1958; "Wipe Out Savage Street Gangs," editorial, *Philadelphia Inquirer*, April 29, 1958.

21. "Youth Crime and Punishment," editorial, *Philadelphia Inquirer*, May 28, 1958; John Calpin, "City Stirred by Negro Crime," *Sunday Bulletin*, May 4, 1958.

22. Marilyn Steinberg to Mayor Richardson Dilworth, n.d., File Korean Incident, Box A 4400, Mayor Files, 1958, Municipal Developments (A-R), Philadelphia Municipal Archives (PMA).

23. David Malis to Richardson Dilworth, May 1, 1958, Korean Incident, PMA.

24. Mrs. M. Rafferty to Richardson Dilworth, May 5, 1958, Korean Incident, PMA.

25. Dorothy Ciperson to Mayor Dilworth, May 1, 1958, Korean Incident, PMA.

26. Haywood Wiley to Mayor Dilworth, May 1, 1958, Korean Incident, PMA.

27. Cerela Shockley to Mayor Dilworth, October 26, 1958, Crime Situation, PMA. See the additional letters in both files as well as in Juvenile (Correspondence from Citizens).

28. "None of 11 Suspects Should Go Free, Citizens Tell Reporters," *Philadelphia Tribune*, May 6, 1958; "Tuscan-Morning Star Lodge Aiding Fight on Juvenile Delinquency; Tribune Editor and DA Blanc Urge Tough Policy at Banquet," *Philadelphia Tribune*, May 20, 1958; "Beyond the Pale," editorial, *Philadelphia Tribune*, October 21, 1958. Philadelphia was not the only place where African Americans pressed for tougher police policies. See Michael Javen Fortner, *Black Silent Majority: The Rockefeller Drug Laws and the Politics of Punishment* (Cambridge, MA: Harvard University Press, 2015).

29. The *Tribune* published a number of articles comparing the treatment of the eleven defendants in the In-Ho Oh case with that of white teenagers who attacked either African Americans or other whites. See "Blast Coddling of Girl's Killer; Racial Distinction in the Treatment of Criminals Hit," June 9, 1959; "Court Rules Cooney Lad 'Confused,' Immature Child," June 23, 1959; "Victims Near Death Following Beating by So. Philly Gang," August 29, 1959; and "All Must Share Blame for Senseless Schoolboy Murder," March 2, 1960.

30. "Parents of Youths Shocked, Saddened by Brutal Killing," *Philadelphia Tribune*, May 3, 1958.

31. "Policy of the Powelton Village Development Associates, Inc. to the Neighborhood Committee and Other Reviewers," Powelton Village Development Association (PVDA) Papers, TUA; "Powelton Village Yesterday and Today," n.d., PVDA Papers, TUA; folder Community Organization Proposals, Box 7, PVDA Papers, TUA; "Powelton Village: Paradise in the City," *Pittsburgh Courier*, October 22, 1960, folder Newspaper Clippings, Box 7, PVDA Papers, TUA; Kirk R. Petshek, *The Challenge of Urban Reform: Policies and Programs in Philadelphia* (Philadelphia: Temple University Press, 1973), 248–49.

32. "Report of the Information and Promotion Committee," Board meeting, August 5, 1958, folder Committee and Other Reports, Box 10, PVDA Papers, TUA.

33. "46 Letters Sent to Gibbons on Slaying," *Philadelphia Evening Bulletin*, May 5, 1958; Thomas Curran to District Attorney Victor Blanc, n.d., Korean Incident, PMA.

34. "Penn Area Slaying Sparks Angry Rally," *Daily News*, April 28, 1958; "Brash Teens Raid Crime Fighters," *Philadelphia Daily News*, May 1, 1958; "Residents Pledged Aid by Gibbons," *Philadelphia Evening Bulletin*, April 29, 1958; "Integrated Private Housing Works, A Vicious Crime Failed to Disunite Residents of Powelton Village," *Pittsburgh Courier*, October 3, 1959, folder Newspaper Clippings, Box 7, PVDA Papers, TUA.

35. For a discussion of why officials in New York played down racial conflict, a pattern I also discuss in *Vampires*, see Robert W. Snyder, "A Useless and Terrible Death: The Michael Farmer Case, 'Hidden Violence,' and New York City in the Fifties," *Journal of Urban History* 36 (March 2010): 226–50. Philadelphia officialdom reacted very differently to the Oh case.

36. Matthew J. Countryman, *Up South: Civil Rights and Black Power in Philadelphia* (Philadelphia: University of Pennsylvania Press, 2006), chap. 1; James Wolfinger, *Philadelphia Divided: Race and Politics in the City of Brotherly Love* (Chapel Hill: University of North Carolina Press, 2007), 198–202, 217–18.

37. "Mayor Blames Both Races in Crime Upsurge," *Philadelphia Evening Bulletin*, May 5, 1958.

38. "Draft of Television Talk on Juvenile Situation," Juvenile Planning, PMA; "Mayor Blames Both Races in Crime Upsurge," *Philadelphia Evening Bulletin*, May 5, 1958; "Dilworth Sees Lack of State Teen Institutions," *Philadelphia Inquirer*, May 17, 1958; "Dilworth Rejects Harshness in Dealing with Delinquents," *Philadelphia Evening Bulletin*, May 27, 1958; "Mayor Asks Co-operation in Drive Against Crime," *Philadelphia Evening Bulletin*, May 5, 1958.

39. Elizabeth Hartopp to Mayor Dilworth, May 8, 1958, Juvenile (Correspondence from Citizens), PMA.

40. Alison Isenberg, *Downtown America: A History of the Place and the People Who Made it* (Chicago: University of Chicago Press, 2004).

41. Commission on Human Relations, "Urban Renewal and Intergroup Relations" (December 1959), Folder 148.4, Commission on Human Relations, Annual Reports and Reports, Box A 620, PMA. For background on the commission, see Pedro A. Regaldo, "Fair Housing," *Encyclopedia of Greater Philadelphia*, https://philadelphiaencyclopedia.org/archive/fair-housing/.

42. "Phila. Mayor Weeps at Rite for Victim of Young Gang," *New York Herald Tribune*, April 30, 1958; "Murder: Stranger from Afar," *Newsweek*, May 12, 1958; "Hands Dripping Blood," *Time*, May 12, 1958; "Philadelphia's New Problem," *Time*, February 24, 1958.

43. Memorandum from Martin Meyerson to G. Holmes Perkins, Re: Future of the University of Pennsylvania Neighborhood, June 30, 1956, folder Community Relations, West Philadelphia Corporation I, Box 73, UPA 4, Office of the President Records, 1946–1970, Gaylord Harnwell Administration, UPA. (Hereafter records from the Harnwell Administration are cited as UPA 4.)

44. Petshek, *Challenge of Urban Reform*, 92–93.

45. O'Mara, *Cities of Knowledge*, 155–57; Sudow, "Displacement Demonized?" chap. 1; Scott Cohen, "Urban Renewal in West Philadelphia: An Examination of the University of Pennsylvania's Planning, Expansion, and Community Role from the Mid-1940s to the Mid-1970s," History honors thesis, University of Pennsylvania, 1998.

46. Trustees of the University of Pennsylvania, Minutes, May 27, 1958, UPA.

47. Trustees of the University of Pennsylvania, Minutes, January 16, 1959, UPA.

48. Crime Prevention Association of Philadelphia, "An Adventure in Human Understanding: The Crime Prevention Association, 1932–1969" (Philadelphia, 1969), 10; Brown, *Law Administration and Negro-White Relations*, 76. For coverage in the *Philadelphia Tribune*, see "Model Boy Shot to Death in Gang Fight over Girls," April 4, 1940; "Community Center Need of West Phila. Youth," April 18, 1940; "Bullet Punctured West Philly 'Gang War' Told in Pictures," October 3, 1940; "5 More Gang Members Held in Feud Probe," November 4, 1944; "Gang Warfare Flares in West Section of City," March 10, 1945; "Young Thugs Renew Rival Gang Warfare," June 9, 1945; "The Tops and the Bottoms," August 4, 1945; "Crippled Youth Badly Injured As 'Tops' and 'Bottoms' Gangs Flare-Up," July 2, 1949; and "Police Halt Clash of Tops and Bottoms," November 27, 1951.

49. Finn Hornum, "Crime and Delinquency in an Area of West Philadelphia" (Philadelphia: University of Pennsylvania, 1963), 53–56. In Hornum's survey, nearly 60 percent of the victims of crime (of all sorts) known to police were white. Both O'Mara (*Cities of Knowledge*) and Hirsch (*Making the Second Ghetto*) underplay the seriousness of crime in motivating university efforts to remake their environs.

50. Marketers Research Service, Inc., "A Profile of Basic Market Factors in the West Philadelphia Corporation Market Area," Table 1, folder West Philadelphia Corporation IV, Box 74, UPA 4.

51. Audrey J. Maetzold, Tenth Annual Report on Social Planning in West Area, Philadelphia District Health and Welfare Council, "A Socio-Geographic Report: The City West of the Schuylkill, April 1954–55," Health and Welfare Council Records, TUA.

52. Marvin Wolfgang, "Brief Proposal for a Study of Crime and Delinquency in University City," folder Community Relations I, 1960–65, Box 152, UPA 4; Conrad Weiler, *Philadelphia: Neighborhood, Authority, and the Urban Crisis* (New York: Praeger, 1974), 112–14, 134–35; John B. Collins, "Relocation of Negroes Displaced by Urban Renewal Projects with Emphasis on the Philadelphia Experience," master's thesis, Wharton School, University of Pennsylvania, 1961.

53. Philadelphia Housing Association, *Relocation in Philadelphia* (Philadelphia, 1958), 8–12; 42.

54. O'Mara, *Cities of Knowledge*, chap. 4.

55. Powelton Village Homeowners Association, "Statement on Renewal Plans for Area III," folder: Community Relations-West Phil. Corp. Powelton Village Homeowners Association, 1960–65, Box 154, UPA 4.

56. Trustees of the University of Pennsylvania, Minutes, October 16, 1959, UPA. On crime in Powelton, Henry Henninger to Police Commissioner Brown, November 6, 1960, folder Community Relations, 1960–65, Box 152, UPA 4; Petshek, *Challenge of Urban Reform*, 247–48.

57. Maj Ellen Borei, "The Challenge of the City to the Church: A Study of One Inner City Church" master's thesis, University of Pennsylvania, 1966, 7–18; Strategy Committee, Presbytery of Philadelphia, "Report on West Philadelphia, South of Market Street," n.d., Tabernacle Presbyterian Church, Community Center Coordinating Committee, Minutes, 1959–1965; Tabernacle Presbyterian Church, Session Minutes, vol. 4 (1956–1965), May 7, 1958; "Background for Action: Historical Sketch Including Recent Involvement Tabernacle Church Presbyterian and United Church of Christ," pamphlet collection, Tabernacle United Church Records, c. 1950–1985, Presbyterian Historical Society, Philadelphia; Mackenzie S. Carlson, "'Come to Where the Knowledge Is': A History of the University City Science Center," http://www.archives.upenn.edu/histy/features/upwphil/ucscpart3.html.

58. The story is well told in O'Mara, *Cities of Knowledge*, 175–79; Jonathan Goldstein, "Vietnam Research on Campus: The Summit/Spicerack Controversy at the University of Pennsylvania," *Peace and Change* 11 (July 1986): 27–49; and Jimmy Tobias, "Military-Academic Complex," *34th Street*, December 3, 2009.

59. Guian A. McKee, *The Problem of Jobs: Liberalism, Race and Deindustrialization in Philadelphia* (Chicago: University of Chicago Press, 2008).

60. Petshek, *Challenge of Urban Reform*, 242–47; Gregory L. Heller, *Ed Bacon: Planning, Politics, and the Building of Modern Philadelphia* (Philadelphia: University of Pennsylvania Press, 2013).

61. See O'Mara, *Cities of Knowledge.*

62. Jessica Lee Oliff, "University City High School: An Experiment in Innovative Education, 1959–1972," History honors thesis, University of Pennsylvania, 2000.

63. Charles Biddle to Gaylord Harnwell, October 10, 1958, folder In-Ho Oh, Alumni Records Collection, UPA.

64. "Parents Unable to Heal Murder Scars," *Philadelphia Evening Bulletin*, April 2, 1967; "2 Convicted in Mugging of Officer," *Philadelphia Evening Bulletin*, November 28, 1979.

65. Ki Byung Oh and Shin Hyn Oh to Gaylord Harnwell, May 2, 1958, folder In-Ho Oh, Alumni Records Collection, UPA.

66. "Parents Unable to Heal Murder Scars," *Philadelphia Evening Bulletin*, April 2, 1967.

67. Sudow, "Displacement Demonized?"

## Chapter 4

1. *Philadelphia Tribune*, September 1, 1964; *Chicago Tribune*, August 30, 1964.

2. Cheryl Lynn Greenberg, *Or Does It Explode: Black Harlem in the Great Depression* (New York: Oxford University Press, 1991).

3. Lenora E. Berson, *Case Study of a Riot: The Philadelphia Story* (New York: Institute of Human Relations Press, 1966), 103.

4. G. Gordon Brown, *Law Administration and Negro-White Relations in Philadelphia: A Study in Race Relations* (Philadelphia: Bureau of Municipal Research of Philadelphia, 1947), 100–22. For composition of the Philadelphia Police Department and the survey of attitudes, see Harlan Hahn and Judson L. Jeffries, *Urban America and Its Police: From the Postcolonial Era to the Turbulent 1960s* (Boulder: University Press of Colorado, 2003), 126. Karl E. Johnson, "Police-Black Community Relations in Postwar Philadelphia: Race and Criminalization in Urban Social Spaces, 1945–1960," *Journal of African American History* 89 (Spring 2004): 118–34; *Philadelphia Tribune*, June 7, 1960; Matthew J. Countryman, *Up South: Civil Rights and Black Power in Philadelphia* (Philadelphia: University of Pennsylvania Press, 2006), 154–55.

5. Participants are quoted in the *Philadelphia Tribune*, September 1, 1964.

6. *Philadelphia Tribune*, September 1, 1964; Berson, *Case Study of a Riot*, 15–20; Countryman, *Up South*, 155–57. Alex Elkins, "Columbia Avenue Riot," *Encyclopedia of Greater Philadelphia*, http://philadelphiaencyclopedia.org/archive/columbia-avenue-riot/. On characterizations of the crowd as young and lower class, see Nicole Maurantonio, "Standing By: Police Paralysis, Race, and the 1964 Philadelphia Riot," *Journalism History* 38 (Summer 2012): 110–21. This was also a trope used by more middle-class blacks to distance themselves from the looters.

7. *Philadelphia Tribune*, September 1, 1964.

8. Countryman, *Up South*, 162–64; S. A. Paolantonio, *Frank Rizzo: The Last Big Man in Big City America* (Philadelphia: Camino, 1993), 76; Frank Donner, *Protectors of Privilege: Red Squads and Police Repression in Urban America* (Berkeley: University of California Press, 1990), chap. 6; Joseph R. Daughen and Peter Binzen, *The Cop Who Would Be King: Mayor Frank Rizzo* (Boston: Little, Brown, 1977), chap. 9; Fred J. Hamilton, *Rizzo* (New York: Viking, 1973), 73–75; H. G. Bissinger, "On Police, a Look at the Records of Goode and Rizzo," *Philadelphia Inquirer*, October 11, 1987.

9. Hahn and Jeffries, *Urban America and Its Police*; Robert M. Fogelson, *Violence as Protest: A Study of Riots and Ghettos* (Garden City, NY: Doubleday, 1971); Thomas J. Sugrue,

*Sweet Land of Liberty: The Forgotten Struggle for Civil Rights in the North* (New York: Random House, 2008); Leonard N. Moore, *Black Rage in New Orleans: Police Brutality and African American Activism from World War II to Hurricane Katrina* (Baton Rouge: Louisiana State University Press, 2010); Countryman, *Up South*; Dwight Watson, *Race and the Houston Police Department, 1930–1990* (College Station: Texas A&M University Press, 2005); Patrick D. Jones, *The Selma of the North: Civil Rights Insurgency in Milwaukee* (Cambridge, MA: Harvard University Press, 2009); Tera Agyepong, "In the Belly of the Beast: Black Policemen Combat Police Brutality in Chicago, 1968–1983," *Journal of African American History* 98 (Spring 2013): 253–76.

10. Martha Biondi, *To Stand and Fight: The Struggle for Civil Rights in Postwar New York City* (Cambridge, MA: Harvard University Press, 2003); Moore, *Black Rage in New Orleans*, 55–57, 126–28; Watson, *Race and the Houston Police Department*, 127; *Report of the National Advisory Commission on Civil Disorders* (New York: Bantam, 1968), 310–11.

11. With few exceptions, the PAB has been ignored by historians: see Countryman, *Up South*; Maurantonio, "Standing By"; and Timothy J. Lombardo, *Blue-Collar Conservatism: Frank Rizzo's Philadelphia and the Politics of the Urban Crisis* (Philadelphia: University of Pennsylvania Press, 2018). Samuel Walker has a brief account in *Police Accountability: The Role of Citizen Oversight* (Belmont, CA: Wadsworth , 2001), 23–25. For the New York City Review Board, see Michael W. Flamm, "'Law and Order' at Large: The New York Civilian Review Board Referendum of 1966 and the Crisis of Liberalism," *Historian* 64, no. 3–4 (2002): 643–65; and Marilynn S. Johnson, *Street Justice: A History of Police Violence in New York City* (Boston: Beacon, 2003), chap. 7. For the background of the Philadelphia board, see A. Alexander Morisey Jr., "The Philadelphia Police Advisory Board," master's thesis, University of Pennsylvania, 1963, 10–12; and Spencer Coxe, "Police Advisory Board: The Philadelphia Story," *Connecticut Bar Journal* 35 (1961): 138–55. Coxe was the executive director of the Philadelphia ACLU, where he began in 1952.

12. Themis Chronopoulos, "Police Misconduct, Community Opposition, and Urban Governance in New York City, 1945–1965," *Journal of Urban History* 44 (July 2018), 645; Marcy S. Sacks, "'To Show Who Was in Charge': Police Repression of New York City's Black Population at the Turn of the Twentieth Century," *Journal of Urban History* 31 (September 2005): 799–815; Simon Ezra Balto, "'Occupied Territory': Police Repression and Black Resistance in Postwar Milwaukee, 1950–1968," *Journal of African American History* 98 (Spring 2013): 229–52; Leanne C. Serbulo and Karen J. Gibson, "Black and Blue: Police-Community Relations in Portland's Albina District, 1964–1985," *Oregon Historical Quarterly* 114 (January 2013): 6–37.

13. The Police Advisory Board records, cited below, are in the Mercer Tate Papers at the Temple University Urban Archives as part of Temple's Special Collections Research Center. The record of complaints and resolutions is incomplete, but when supplemented by letters, memoranda, newspaper clippings, and the like, they give a reasonably full picture both of the operations of the PAB and the nature of the complaints received. While there is a risk in extrapolating from these complaints to a broader argument about police-community relations—the board collected complaints about police, not encomiums—the sources together fit with both historical and contemporary analyses of policing in inner-city communities.

14. Lee Rainwater, "Revolt of the Dirty Workers," *Society* 5 (November 1967): 2. Rainwater borrowed the term from Everett C. Hughes and applied it to a U.S. context. Hughes, "Good People and Dirty Work," *Social Problems* 10 (Summer 1962: 3–11.

15. Johnson, *Street Justice*, passim; Johnson, "Police-Black Community Relations," 123–27; Balto, "'Occupied Territory,'" 234–36; Cathy Lisa Schneider, *Police Power and Race Riots: Urban Unrest in Paris and New York* (Philadelphia: University of Pennsylvania Press, 2014), 5. On the influence of the racial composition of neighborhoods on policing, see Douglas A. Smith, "The Neighborhood Context of Police Behavior," in *Communities and Crime*, ed. Albert J. Reiss and Michael Tonry (Chicago: University of Chicago Press, 1986), 313–42. On the geographic concentration of crime, see Eric Schneider, *Smack: Heroin and the American City* (Philadelphia: University of Pennsylvania Press, 2008), 116–21.

16. On the difference between the academy and policing on the street, see Peter Moskos, *Cop in the Hood: My Year Policing Baltimore's Eastern District* (Princeton: Princeton University Press, 2008); and Jonathan Rubinstein, *City Police* (New York: Farrar, Straus & Giroux, 1973). See also Balto, "'Occupied Territory,'" 234–37. As an example, see Peter Maas, *Serpico* (New York: Viking, 1973), 154–55. Thanks to Will Cooley for this reference. For contemporary studies of the social ecology of policing, see William Terrill and Michael D. Reisig, "Neighborhood Context and Police Use of Force," *Journal of Research in Crime and Delinquency* 40 (August 2003): 291–321.

17. For ethnic composition of police, see Arthur Niederhoffer, *Behind the Shield: Police in Urban Society* (Garden City, NY: Anchor, 1969). On the link between police and white ethnic neighborhoods, see Lombardo, *Blue-Collar Conservatism*, chap. 1.

18. John M. McLarnon and G. Terry Madonna, "Dilworth, Clark, and Reform in Philadelphia, 1947–1962," *Pennsylvania Legacies* 11 (November 2011): 24–31; Peter Binzen, *Richardson Dilworth: The Last of the Bare-Knuckled Aristocrats* (Philadelphia: Camino, 2014), chap. 12; Pedro A. Regalado, "Fair Housing," *Encyclopedia of Greater Philadelphia*, http://philadelphiaencyclopedia.org/archive/fair-housing/; Guian A. McKee, *The Problem of Jobs: Liberalism, Race, and Deindustrialization in Philadelphia* (Chicago: University of Chicago Press, 2008), 18–22.

19. Binzen, *Dilworth*, 112–13; Matthew J. Countryman, "'From Protest to Politics': Community Control and Black Independent Politics in Philadelphia, 1965–1984," *Journal of Urban History* 32 (September 2006): 813–61. On opposition to integration as a source of discord in the New Deal coalition, see Thomas J. Sugrue, *The Origins of the Urban Crisis: Race and Inequality in Postwar Detroit* (Princeton: Princeton University Press, 1996); and Sugrue, "Crabgrass-Roots Politics: Race, Rights, and the Reaction Against Liberalism in the Urban North, 1940–1964," *Journal of American History* 82 (September 1995): 551–78.

20. Coxe, "Police Advisory Board," 139–42; Binzen, *Dilworth*, 104, 198; Robert J. Bray Jr., "Police: Philadelphia's Police Advisory Board— A New Concept in Community Relations," *Villanova Law Review* 7 (1962): 656–73; Stephen C. Halpern, "Police Employee Organizations and Accountability Procedures in Three Cities: Some Reflections on Police Policy-Making," *Law and Society Review* 8 (Summer 1974): 561–82.

21. Bray, "Philadelphia's Police Advisory Board," 658.

22. Letter from Mercer Tate to Maurice Fagan, Fellowship Commission, July 31, 1969, PAB, Box 1, Temple University Urban Archives (TUA). The names of complainants and police officers are indicated using the first initial of the last name and ellipses (unless they are part of the public record), and I have not used file names since they frequently contain the names of complainants, as per agreement with TUA.

23. PAB, Annual Report, 1960, Box A-191, Mayor, Misc. Annual Reports, Philadelphia City Archives (PCA). Hereafter cited only by date. Coxe, "Police Advisory Board," 152–53; Halpern, "Police Employee Organizations," 563.

24. Fraternal Order of Police, Committee on Human Rights and Law Enforcement, "Police Review Boards: A Threat to Law Enforcement" (Philadelphia, 1962).

25. Halpern, "Police Employee Organizations," 563.

26. Spencer Coxe, "The Philadelphia Police Advisory Board," *Law in Transition Quarterly* 2, no. 3 (1965): 179–85; PAB, Annual Report, 1961.

27. Bray, "Philadelphia's Police Advisory Board," 661; Coxe, "Philadelphia Police Advisory Board," 180–81.

28. Gibbons is quoted in Coxe, "Police Advisory Board," 153.

29. James R. Hudson, "The Civilian Review Board Issue as Illuminated by the Philadelphia Experience," *Criminology* 6 (November 1968): 16–29; *Philadelphia Tribune*, August 8, 1964.

30. Coxe, "Police Advisory Board," 150–51; Carl Werthman and Irving Piliavin, "Gang Members and the Police," in *The Police: Six Sociological Essays*, ed. David J. Bordua (New York: Wiley, 1967): 56–98.

31. Bray, "Philadelphia Police Advisory Board," 663–64; PAB, Annual Report, 1959, 1960, and 1961. On problems arising from the use of public space and amusement parks, see Sugrue, *Sweet Land of Liberty*, 152–59.

32. Affidavit from Mercer Tate, *Alexander, et al. v. Rizzo et al.,* PAB, Box 3.

33. Bray, "Philadelphia Police Advisory Board," 663–65.

34. Affidavit from DW, *Alexander et al. v. Rizzo et al.*, PAB, Box 3; Joseph D. Lohman and Gordon E. Misner, *The Police and the Community: The Dynamics of Their Relationship in a Changing Society* (Washington, DC: President's Commission on Law Enforcement and Administration of Justice, 1966), 121–29; Werthman and Piliavin, "Gang Members and the Police," 56–57.

35. Correspondence, Chairman, Feb.–June, 1963, case 314, PAB, Box 1; Rubinstein, *City Police*, 249; Hahn and Jeffries, *Urban America and Its Police*, chap. 2; James R. Hudson, "Police-Citizen Encounters That Lead to Citizen Complaints," *Social Problems* 18 (Autumn 1970): 179–93; for a spatial argument on the location of drug markets, see Schneider, *Smack*, and on vice, see Sacks, "'To Show Who Was in Charge,'" 811–13.

36. Letter from Mercer Tate to Mayor James Tate, May 29, 1967, Correspondence, Chairman, 1967, PAB, Box 1.

37. Correspondence, Chairman, Feb.–June, 1963, case 317, PAB, Box 1; Letter from William Gray to Mayor James Tate, July 15, 1964, PAB, Box 1.

38. Correspondence, Chairman, Feb.–June, 1963, cases 312, 333, and 319, PAB, Box 1.

39. Schneider, *Smack*, chap. 6; Rubinstein, *City Police*, chap. 9; Chronopoulos, "Police Misconduct."

40. For a contemporary account of police practice in serving warrants in Philadelphia, see Alice Goffman, *On the Run: Fugitive Life in an American City* (Chicago: University of Chicago Press, 2014).

41. Opinion, complaint of Ronald R and Maxine R against Policemen B and S, PAB, Box 3.

42. Letter from Mercer Tate to Mayor James Tate, May 29, 1967, PAB, Box 1; Hudson, "Civilian Review Board Issue," 22. On the commonplace nature of these complaints in black communities, see Hahn and Jeffries, *Urban America and Its Police*, 111–16.

43. Rubinstein, *City Police*, chap. 7; Hahn and Jeffries, *Urban America and Its Police*, chap. 3; Fogelson, *Violence as Protest*, 55–60; Lohman and Misner, *Police and the Community*,

121–29, 142–53; David Kairys, *Philadelphia Freedom: Memoir of a Civil Rights Lawyer* (Ann Arbor: University of Michigan Press, 2008), 146–51, 155–61. The case files in box 3 of the PAB records are full of reports of incidents, mostly car stops, escalating into physical confrontations even when complainants did not offer any initial physical resistance to interrogation.

44. PAB, Annual Report, 1959, 5; Johnson, *Street Justice*, 252–53; United States Commission on Civil Rights, *Police Practices and Civil Rights: Hearings Held in Philadelphia, Pennsylvania, February 6, 1979; April 16–17, 1979* (Washington, DC, 1979), 47.

45. Rubinstein, *City Police*, 183; Johnson, *Street Justice*, 243–44; Christopher Lowen Agee, *The Streets of San Francisco: Policing and the Creation of a Cosmopolitan Liberal Politics, 1950–1972* (Chicago: University of Chicago Press, 2014); Hahn and Jeffries, *Urban America and Its Police*, 88–92.

46. Opinion, Complaint of Mrs. Marie R and George M Against Sgt. Donald C, Policeman John Q, and Policeman Peter E, PAB, Box 1. See also Letter from William Gray to Mayor James Tate, June 16, 1964, PAB, Box 1.

47. *New York Times*, July 24, 1964, in which CORE called the PAB useless.

48. PAB, Annual Report, 1966, Appendix D; Countryman, *Up South*, 283–84; Lohman and Misner, *Police and the Community*, 213–23.

49. *Philadelphia Tribune*, August 8, 1964, on Freeman; "Why Do Police Fear Advisory Board?" *Philadelphia Tribune*, October 1, 1966; "Can Police Really Police Policemen?" *Philadelphia Tribune*, April 4, 1967; *Philadelphia Tribune*, April 29, 1967.

50. On support for police, especially by middle-class blacks, see Michael Javen Fortner, *The Black Silent Majority: The Rockefeller Drug Laws and the Politics of Punishment* (Cambridge, MA: Harvard University Press, 2015); Chronopoulos, "Police Misconduct," 654; Moore, *Black Rage in New Orleans*, 4.

51. Countryman, *Up South*, 149–52; Sugrue, *Sweet Land of Liberty*, 320–22; Balto, "'Occupied Territory.'"

52. Halpern, "Police Employee Organizations," 568, quotes Hoover.

53. *Philadelphia Bulletin*, September 7, 1965, newspaper clippings, 1959–69, PAB, Box 2.

54. John Harrington, WCAU editorial, September 28, 1965, newspaper clippings, 1959–69, PAB, Box 2.

55. Maurantonio, "Standing By," 114–15.

56. *Philadelphia Bulletin*, September 7, 1965; *Philadelphia Inquirer*, October 19, 1966; newspaper clippings, 1959–65, PAB, Box 2; Halpern, "Police Employee Organizations," 563–64; Coxe, "Philadelphia Police Advisory Board," 183; Countryman, *Up South*, 162–64.

57. Letter from Spence Coxe to the *Philadelphia Inquirer*, November 2, 1966, Correspondence, Chairman, 1966, PAB, Box 1.

58. Johnson, *Street Justice*, chap. 7; Flamm, "'Law and Order' at Large," 652–61. Fortner shows that opposition to the board among whites varied by religion and class and rejects the notion of a uniform white backlash. See *Black Silent Majority*, 227–28.

59. These are my calculations based on the FBI Uniform Crime Reports. Crime statistics are a better measure of police activity than they are of crime and have been justly criticized for overemphasizing and reinforcing notions of black criminality. See Khalil Gibran Muhammad, *The Condemnation of Blackness: Race, Crime, and the Making of Modern Urban America* (Cambridge, MA: Harvard University Press, 2010); and Elizabeth Hinton, *From the War on Poverty to the War on Crime: The Making of Mass Incarceration in America* (Cambridge, MA:

Harvard University Press, 2016). However, a murder produces an artifact that has to be accounted for, and while there may be some misclassifications and errors, the murder rate is a solid measure of the most lethal form of violence. It is significant that the nation's largest cities show an increase in murder starting around 1960, which belies the argument that crime rates did not rise in the early 1960s. On the latter, see Hinton, *From the War on Poverty to the War on Crime*; and Heather Ann Thompson, "Why Mass Incarceration Matters: Rethinking Crisis, Decline, and Transformation in Postwar American History," *Journal of American History* 97 (December 2010): 703–34. My sample of murders in Philadelphia shows significant geographic concentration of homicides in three black neighborhoods for the 1940s to 1960s. See Marvin Wolfgang, *Patterns in Criminal Homicide* (Philadelphia: University of Pennsylvania Press, 1958), 32–33; he found that for 1948 to 1952, a period of low homicide rates nationally, the homicide rate in Philadelphia was 1.9 per 100,000 for whites compared with 22.5 per 100,000 for blacks.

60. *Philadelphia Bulletin*, January 11, 1966; Letter from Mercer Tate to Mayor James Tate, Ninth Annual Report, 1967, PAB, Box 1; Fellowship Commission, Committee on Community Tensions, Minutes, January 7, 1966, PAB, Box 2.

61. *Philadelphia Bulletin*, July 24, 1968; Lombardo in *Blue-Collar Conservatism*, chap. 2, has a more sympathetic view of Tate.

62. U.S. Commission on Civil Rights, *Police Practices*, 245.

63. *Philadelphia Tribune*, July 12, 1969.

64. Reinstatement of the Police Advisory Board, Press Release, July 2, 1969; Letter from Mercer Tate to Mayor James Tate, September 4, 1969; Correspondence, chairman, 1969, PAB, Box 1; *Philadelphia Tribune*, September 13, 1969.

65. *Philadelphia Tribune*, December 13, 1969.

66. *Philadelphia Tribune*, December 23, 1969.

67. Hearing of the [Medical] Examiner, 1966, PAB, Box 2.

68. *Philadelphia Tribune*, December 23, 1969.

69. The Police Advisory Commission was established in 1993 by Mayor Edward Rendell.

70. Paolantonio, *Frank Rizzo*; Daughen and Binzen, *Cop Who Would Be King*; Lombardo, *Blue-Collar Conservatism*, chap. 5.

71. Michelle Alexander, *The New Jim Crow: Mass Incarceration in the Age of Colorblindness* (New York: New Press, 2010).

72. U.S. Department of Justice, Special Litigation Section, https://www.justice.gov/crt/special-litigation-section-cases-and-matters0#police.

73. Walker, *Police Accountability*, 6; Joe Domanick, *Blue: The LAPD and the Battle to Reform American Policing* (New York: Simon & Schuster, 2015). In Philadelphia, the FOP has resisted the Police Advisory Commission with the same vigor that it resisted the PAB, and critiques of the commission that it fails to protect citizens from police brutality are similar to criticism of the PAB. See Human Rights Watch, *Shielded from Justice: Police Brutality and Accountability in the United States* (1998), "Philadelphia: Police Advisory Commission," https://www.hrw.org/legacy/reports98/police/uspo110.htm; Michael Coard, "Can Citizens Keep Philly Cops in Line?" *Philadelphia Magazine*, February 17, 2012.

74. James Baldwin, "Fifth Avenue, Uptown," *Esquire*, July 1960, http://www.esquire.com/news-politics/a3638/fifth-avenue-uptown/.

Chapter 5

1. Pennsylvania Economy League, *The Gang Problem in Philadelphia: Proposals for Improving the Programs of Gang-Control Agencies* (Philadelphia, 1974), 14; S. A. Paolantonio, *Frank Rizzo: The Last Big Man in Big City America* (Philadelphia: Camino, 1993).

2. *Philadelphia Bulletin*, August 13, 1969.

3. Joseph Daughen and Peter Binzen, *The Cop Who Would Be King: Mayor Frank Rizzo* (Boston: Little, Brown, 1977), chap. 10; Paolantonio, *Frank Rizzo*, 130.

4. Bruce Laurie, "Fire Companies and Gangs in Southwark: The 1840s," in *The Peoples of Philadelphia: A History of Ethnic Groups and Lower-Class Life, 1790–1940*, ed. Allen F. Davis and Mark H. Haller (Philadelphia: Temple University Press, 1973), 71–83; David Montgomery, "The Shuttle and the Cross: Weavers and Artisans in the Kensington Riots of 1844," *Journal of Social History* 5 (Summer 1972): 411–46.

5. Pennsylvania Crime Commission, "A Report on the Inquiry into Gang Violence in Philadelphia," July 31, 1969, 9, 18.

6. Lateef Fattah is quoted in Robert L. Woodson, *A Summons to Life: Mediating Structures and the Prevention of Youth Crime* (Cambridge: Ballinger, 1981), 65; *Philadelphia Bulletin*, May 14 and May 15, 1970.

7. Gerald D. Robin, "Gang Member Delinquency: Its Extent, Sequence and Typology," *The Journal of Criminal Law, Criminology, and Police Science*, 55 (March, 1964): 59–69; Barry Alan Krisberg, "Urban Leadership Training: An Ethnographic Study of 22 Gang Leaders," (PhD diss., University of Pennsylvania, 1971), 176–86; *Philadelphia Bulletin*, May 20, 1964; *Philadelphia Inquirer*, November 29, 1972. For a series on "the Jungle," see *Philadelphia Bulletin*, February 3, 17, and 23, 1957.

8. *Philadelphia Bulletin*, May 25, 1969; *Philadelphia Inquirer*, August 24, 1969; Select Committee on Crime, House of Representatives, *Crime in America: Youth Gang Warfare* (Washington, D.C., 1970), 13, 30, 161; *Philadelphia Bulletin*, June 25, 1969.

9. Nancy Loving, "Somerville in the Streets," *Community Forum* (Spring 1970): 1–3, 11; Police Advisory Board Records, Series II, Box 2, File LaSalle College, Urban Studies and Community Services Center, 1969–1970, Temple University Urban Archives.

10. George D. Newton and Franklin Zimring, *Firearms and Violence in American Life; A Staff Report Submitted to the National Commission on the Causes and Prevention of Violence* (Washington, D.C., 1968), 18–19; *Philadelphia Inquirer*, November 29, 1972.

11. Carl Husemoller Nightingale, *On the Edge: A History of Poor Black Children and Their American Dreams* (New York: Basic, 1993), 15, 21.

12. *Commonwealth v. Edward Fields*, February Sessions, 1965; *Commonwealth v. Fields*, 463 Pa 244 (Pa 1975).

13. Pennsylvania Crime Commission, "A Report on the Inquiry into Gang Violence," 8. On New York gangs, see Eric C. Schneider, *Vampires, Dragons, and Egyptian Kings: Youth Gangs in Postwar New York* (Princeton: Princeton University Press, 1998).

14. On the impact of breaks, see Grady Clay, *Close-Up: How to Read the American City* (New York: Praeger, 1973). The Rosen Homes were among the first high-rise public housing projects imploded under the U.S. Department of Housing and Urban Development's Hope VI program, which intended to replace such structures with homes open to a greater mix of income among its residents. See syndicated columnist Neal R. Peirce's column, "What Comes After They Dynamite the Public Housing?" *Baltimore Sun*, May 22, 1995.

15. *Philadelphia Inquirer*, May 16, 1971; *Philadelphia Bulletin*, June 23, 1971. For later incidents, see *Philadelphia Bulletin*, March 3, 1972; March 24, 1972; March 26, 1972; June 19, 1979; April 13, 1980; and July 14, 1981; *Philadelphia Daily News*, June 19, 1979.

16. *Philadelphia Daily News*, July 19, 1973; *Philadelphia Bulletin*, April 24, 1972; *Philadelphia Inquirer*, February 16, 1975; Woodson, *Summons to Life*, 76.

17. *Philadelphia Bulletin*, June 10, 1972; and June 11, 1972; Pennsylvania Economy League, *Gang Problem in Philadelphia*, 11.

18. *Philadelphia Bulletin*, December 3, 1972.

19. Select Committee on Crime, *Crime in America*, 66–67; United States Commission on Civil Rights, *Police Practices and Civil Rights: Hearings Held in Philadelphia, Pennsylvania, February 6, 1979; April 16–17, 1979* (Washington, D.C., 1979), 45–48; *Philadelphia Bulletin*, June 26, 1969; *Philadelphia Inquirer*, June 26, 1969.

20. *Philadelphia Bulletin*, October 2, 1969.

21. *Philadelphia Inquirer*, July 15, 1970; and April 8, 1974; *Philadelphia Bulletin*, April 13, 1970; May 5, 1970; June 8, 1970; and July 7, 1970. Pennsylvania Economy League, *Gang Problem in Philadelphia*, chap. 2, provides an overview of the reorganizations of the various street worker projects.

22. *Philadelphia Bulletin*, May 19, 1973.

23. *Philadelphia Bulletin*, August 23, 1974; and August 27, 1974.

24. *Philadelphia Bulletin*, May 20, 1973.

25. V. P. Franklin, "Operation Street Corner: The Wharton Centre and the Juvenile Gang Problem in Philadelphia, 1945–1958," in *W. E. B. DuBois, Race and the City: The Philadelphia Negro and Its Legacy*, ed. Michael B. Katz and Thomas Sugrue (Philadelphia: University of Pennsylvania Press, 1998), 195–218.

26. Directed, written, and acted by teenagers Charlie Davis, David Williams, and Jimmy Robinson, *The Jungle*, can be accessed on YouTube at https://www.youtube.com/watch?v=Jn6Z5sZZMqk.

27. *Philadelphia Bulletin*, June 8, 1969; author interview with Harold Haskins, May 8, 2014; *Commonwealth v. Robert Nixon*, May Sessions, 1969; *Philadelphia Inquirer*, June 27, 1969; Select Committee on Crime, *Crime in America*, 3. See *Philadelphia Bulletin*, May 14, 1971, for the death of another 12th and Oxford member who had run the gang's laundromat and garage. PGW referred to the project as a disaster; see Krisberg, "Urban Leadership Training," 313.

28. *Philadelphia Inquirer*, November 18, 1968.

29. For the college's history, see David A. Canton, "Girard College," Encyclopedia of Greater Philadelphia, https://philadelphiaencyclopedia.org/archive/girard-college/.

30. *Philadelphia Bulletin*, May 1, 1964; July 13, 1967; August 14, 1971; and August 15, 1971; *Philadelphia Inquirer*, July 11, 1965; Matthew J. Countryman, *Up South: Civil Rights and Black Power in Philadelphia* (Philadelphia: University of Pennsylvania Press, 2006), 168–78.

31. *Philadelphia Bulletin*, September 13, 1967; and May 3, 1968.

32. *Philadelphia Inquirer*, August 2, 1971; Countryman, *Up South*, 286–89; Reggie Schell, "A Way to Fight Back," in *They Should Have Served That Cup of Coffee*, ed. Dick Cluster (Boston: South End, 1979), 41–69; Donna Murch, *Living for the City: Migration, Education, and the Rise of the Black Panther Party in Oakland, California* (Chapel Hill: University of North Carolina Press, 2010), 315.

33. *Philadelphia Inquirer*, October 10, 1975; Countryman, *Up South*, 87–90.

34. Paul Washington, *"Other Sheep I Have": The Autobiography of Father Paul M. Washington* (Philadelphia: Temple University Press, 1994), 51, 147–52.

35. *Philadelphia Inquirer*, August 28, 1974; *Philadelphia Daily News*, January 6, 1975; *Parade Magazine*, May 4, 1980.

36. Stephen Satell, *No Gang War in 74* (self-published, Philadelphia, 2008), 166–80; *Philadelphia Daily News*, April 10, 2012.

37. Author interview with Falaka and David Fattah, May 23, 2014; *Philadelphia Bulletin*, December 10, 1972; David Fattah obituary, *Philadelphia Inquirer*, December 12, 2018.

38. *Parade Magazine*, May 4, 1980; *Philadelphia Bulletin*, February 2, 1972; and December 10, 1972; *New York Times*, August 18, 1977; Woodson, *Summons to Life*, chaps. 3 and 4; Fattah interview.

39. *Philadelphia Bulletin*, February 1, 1972; February 10, 1972; and February 11, 1972; Fattah interview.

40. *Philadelphia Bulletin*, April 10, 1972; April 13, 1972; April 24, 1972; and November 24, 1973.

41. *Philadelphia Bulletin*, November 24, 1973; January 2, 1974; and January 12, 1974; *Philadelphia Daily News*, December 26, 1973.

42. *Philadelphia Bulletin*, June 20, 1974; *Philadelphia Inquirer*, May 22, 1976; *New York Times*, August 18, 1977.

43. *Parade Magazine*, May 4, 1980.

44. *Philadelphia Inquirer*, July 17, 1974; August 18, 1975; and October 10, 1975; *Philadelphia Bulletin*, July 30, 1975.

45. Countryman, *Up South*, chap. 7; Lisa Levenstein, *A Movement Without Marches: African American Women and the Politics of Poverty in Postwar Philadelphia* (Chapel Hill: University of North Carolina Press, 2009).

46. *Philadelphia Bulletin*, October 28, 1974; November 2, 1974; and October 10, 1975; *Philadelphia Inquirer*, December 22, 1976; Bennie J. Swans Jr., "Gangbusters! Crisis Intervention Network," *School Safety* 3 (Winter 1985): 12–15.

47. *Philadelphia Bulletin*, July 30, 1978. There were 140,436 ten- to seventeen-year-old males in Philadelphia in 1970 and 109,692 in 1980.

48. *Philadelphia Bulletin*, April 28, 1969; April 13, 1970; June 8, 1970; April 22, 1971; and December 8, 1972; Eric C. Schneider, *Smack: Heroin and the American City* (Philadelphia: University of Pennsylvania Press, 2008), 100–102; Schell, "A Way to Fight Back," 68.

49. *Philadelphia Inquirer*, December 24, 1981.

50. *Philadelphia Bulletin*, November 9, 1981.

51. Paolantonio, *Frank Rizzo*, 315.

## Chapter 6

1. *New York Times*, August 31, 1970; *Philadelphia Daily News*, August 31, 1970; September 1, 1970; *Philadelphia Inquirer*, August 30, 1970; and August 31, 1970; *Chicago Tribune*, August 31, 1970. For a later summary, see *Philadelphia Inquirer*, October 6, 1997.

2. *Philadelphia Inquirer*, July 10, 2016.

3. *Chicago Tribune*, September 1, 1970.

4. Gerald D. Robin, "Justifiable Homicide by Police Officers," *Journal of Criminal Law, Criminology, and Police Science* 54 (June 1963): 231.

5. These are my calculations based on the Officer Down Memorial Page, https://www
.odmp.org/agency/3101-philadelphia-police-department-pennsylvania.

6. Robin, "Justifiable Homicide," 226.

7. Pennsylvania State Committee to the United States Commission on Civil Rights,
"Police Community Relations in Philadelphia: A Report to the United States Commission on
Civil Rights," 1972, 94–98.

8. Public Interest Law Center of Philadelphia, "Deadly Force: Police Use of Firearms
1970–78," (1979), http://www.pilcop.org/reports-studies/#sthash.Oscfy1fi.dpbs, 6–7; Table 1,
p. 14; William B. Waegel, "The Use of Lethal Force by Police: The Effect of Statutory Change,"
*Crime and Delinquency* 30 (January 1984): 121–40.

9. Richard Kania and Wade C. Mackey, "Police Violence as a Function of Community
Characteristics," *Criminology* 15 (May 1977): 27–48; Waegel, "Use of Lethal Force," 133;
David Lester, "The Murder of Police Officers in American Cities," *Criminal Justice and Behavior* 11 (March 1984): 101–13; Arthur L. Kobler, "Figures (and Perhaps Some Facts) on Police
Killing of Civilians in the United States, 1965–1969," *Journal of Social Issues* 31 (Winter 1975):
185–91; Douglas A. Smith, "The Neighborhood Context of Police Behavior," in *Communities
and Crime*, ed. Albert J. Reiss and Michael Tonry (Chicago: University of Chicago Press,
1986), 313–42; William Terrill and Michael D. Reisig, "Neighborhood Context and Police
Use of Force," *Journal of Research in Crime and Delinquency* 40 (August 2003): 291–321.

10. Studies of police-community relations discuss police killings of civilians but do not
consider the intentional killings of police officers. Themis Chronopoulos, "Police Misconduct,
Community Opposition, and Urban Governance in New York City, 1945–1965," *Journal of
Urban History* 44 (July 2018): 643–68; Marcy S. Sacks, " 'To Show Who Was in Charge': Police
Repression of New York City's Black Population at the Turn of the Twentieth Century,"
*Journal of Urban History* 31 (September 2005): 799–815; Simon Ezra Balto, " 'Occupied Territory': Police Repression and Black Resistance in Postwar Milwaukee, 1950–1968," *Journal of
African American History* 98 (Spring 2013): 229–52; Leanne C. Serbulo and Karen J. Gibson,
"Black and Blue: Police-Community Relations in Portland's Albina District, 1964–1985," *Oregon Historical Quarterly* 114 (January 2013): 6–37; Dwight Watson, *Race and the Houston
Police Department, 1930–1990* (College Station: Texas A&M University Press, 2005); Patrick
D. Jones, *The Selma of the North: Civil Rights Insurgency in Milwaukee* (Cambridge, MA:
Harvard University Press, 2009); Tera Agyepong, "In the Belly of the Beast: Black Policemen
Combat Police Brutality in Chicago, 1968–1983," *Journal of African American History* 98
(Spring 2013): 253–76. An exception is Leonard N. Moore, *Black Rage in New Orleans: Police
Brutality and African American Activism from World War II to Hurricane Katrina* (Baton
Rouge: Louisiana State University Press, 2010).

11. On the relationship between political fracture and murder, see Randolph Roth,
*American Homicide* (Cambridge: Belknap, 2009); Jodi M. Brown and Patrick A. Langan,
"Policing and Homicide, 1976–98: Justifiable Homicide by Police, Police Officers Murdered
by Felons," Bureau of Justice Statistics (March 2001); Candice Batton and Steve Wilson,
"Police Murders: An Examination of Historical Trends in the Killing of Law Enforcement
Officer in the United States, 1947 to 1998," *Homicide Studies* 10 (May 2006): 79–97.

12. Jerome H. Skolnick and James J. Fyfe, *Above the Law: Police and the Excessive Use of
Force* (New York: Free Press, 1993), 140. Citing a U.S. Department of Justice report from
1979, Skolnick and Fyfe reported that "while individual Philadelphia cops were no more likely

than New York cops to make arrests or to come face to face with armed people, they were *thirty-seven times* as likely as New York cops to shoot unarmed people who had threatened nobody and who were fleeing from suspected nonviolent crimes."

13. *Philadelphia Daily News*, January 30, 1970; and January 31, 1970.

14. *Alexander et al. v. Rizzo et al.*, Box 3, Police Advisory Board (Philadelphia, Pa.) Records (PAB), Acc. 670, 677, Special Collections Research Center, Temple University Libraries, Philadelphia.

15. *Alexander et al. v. Rizzo et al.*, PAB Records.

16. Police followed a similar practice after the murder of Officer Thomas Trench in the Spring Garden neighborhood in 1985. See *Spring Garden United v. City of Philadelphia*, 614 F. Supp. 1350 (E.D. Pa. 1985).

17. *Philadelphia Tribune*, April 28, 1970.

18. *Philadelphia Daily News*, June 15, 1972; Akinyele Omowale Umoja, "Repression Breeds Resistance: The Black Liberation Army and the Radical Legacy of the Black Panther Party," in *Liberation, Imagination, and the Black Panther Party: A New Look at the Panthers and Their Legacy*, ed. Kathleen Cleaver and George Katsiaficas (New York: Routledge, 2001), 3–19.

19. Russell Shoats, "Black Fighting Formations: Their Strengths, Weaknesses, and Potentialities," in Cleaver and Katsiaficas, *Liberation, Imagination and the Black Panther Party*, 133.

20. *New York Times*, April 7, 1996; Statement of Alvin Joyner, *Commonwealth v. Alvin Joyner*, December Sessions, 1971.

21. *Philadelphia Daily News*, February 2, 1970; April 3, 1970; April 18, 1970; April 21, 1970; and May 22, 1970; Paul Lyons, *The People of This Generation: The Rise and Fall of the New Left in Philadelphia* (Philadelphia: University of Pennsylvania Press, 2003), 187–89.

22. Thomas Watkins, Assistant District Attorney, address to the jury; Testimony of James Harrington; Statement of Alvin Joyner, *Commonwealth v. Alvin Joyner*, December Sessions, 1971.

23. *New York Times*, April 7, 1996; *Philadelphia Inquirer*, October 6, 1997; November 4, 1997; and November 5, 1997.

24. *Commonwealth v. Alvin Joyner*.

25. Lance Hill, *The Deacons for Defense: Armed Resistance and the Civil Rights Movement* (Chapel Hill: University of North Carolina Press, 2004); Robert F. Williams, *Negroes with Guns* (New York: Marzani & Munsell, 1962); Charles Cobb, *This Nonviolent Stuff'll Get You Killed: How Guns Made the Civil Rights Movement Possible* (New York: Basic, 2014); Akbar Muhammad Ahmad, "RAM: The Revolutionary Action Movement," in *Black Power in the Belly of the Beast*, ed. Judson L. Jeffries (Urbana: University of Illinois Press, 2006), 252–80. On police killings, see Umoja, "Repression Breeds Resistance," 12; and William Rosenau, "'Our Backs Are Against the Wall': The Black Liberation Army and Domestic Terrorism in 1970s America," *Studies in Conflict and Terrorism* 36 (2013): 176–92.

26. *Philadelphia Inquirer*, February 21, 1971; and February 22, 1971; *The Daily Intelligencer*, February 22, 1971; *Philadelphia Daily News*, February 25, 1971.

27. Kenyatta is quoted in Tom Fox, "A Time of Testing," *Philadelphia Daily News*, February 22, 1971.

28. Shoats, "Black Fighting Formations," 133.

29. Waegel, "Use of Lethal Force," 123.

30. *Philadelphia Tribune*, June 7, 1960; June 11, 1960; July 9, 1960; July 19, 1960; March 4, 1961; May 30, 1961; and June 10, 1961.

31. Mary Francis Berry, *And Justice for All: The United States Commission on Civil Rights and the Continuing Struggle for Freedom in America* (New York: Knopf, 2009), 155–56.

32. United States Commission on Civil Rights, *Who Is Guarding the Guardians? A Report on Police Practices* (Washington, DC, 1981), 87–88.

33. Skolnick and Fyfe, *Above the Law*, 139–40.

34. *Philadelphia Inquirer*, "The Homicide Files," April 24–27, 1977; *Wilkinson v. Ellis*, 484 F. Supp. 1072 (E.D. Pa. 1980).

35. Jonathan Rubinstein, *City Police* (New York: Farrar, Straus, & Giroux, 1973), 349.

36. The most complete narrative of the shooting is *Philadelphia Inquirer*, August 8, 1978; see also *Philadelphia Inquirer*, July 13, 1978; July 14, 1978; July 23, 1978; and July 31, 1978. More of the police account is in *Philadelphia Bulletin*, November 7, 1978. See also *Philadelphia Tribune*, July 14, 1978; and April 20, 1979.

37. *Philadelphia Tribune*, April 27, 1979; June 20, 1980; and August 29, 1980; *Philadelphia Bulletin*, April 24, 1979; and July 3, 1979; *Philadelphia Daily News*, April 24, 1979.

38. Skolnick and Fyfe, *Above the Law*, passim.

39. Philadelphia Police Study Task Force, "Philadelphia and Its Police: Toward a New Partnership" (Philadelphia, 1987), 17–24.

40. See the Officer Down Memorial Page, https://www.odmp.org/agency/3101-philadel phia-police-department-pennsylvania.

41. See the obituary for Morton Solomon, *Philadelphia Inquirer*, May 2, 2006; Skolnick and Fyfe, *Above the Law*, 141; *Christian Science Monitor*, July 11, 1980.

42. Marcus Anthony Hunter, *Black Citymakers: How the Philadelphia Negro Changed Urban America* (New York: Oxford University Press, 2013).

43. Brown and Langan, "Policing and Homicide," 19–20.

44. Ward Churchill, " 'To Disrupt, Discredit and Destroy': The FBI's Secret War Against the Black Panther Party," in Cleaver and Katsiaficas, *Liberation, Imagination, and the Black Panther Party*, 78–117; Judson L. Jeffries, "An Unexamined Chapter of Black Panther History," in Jeffries, *Black Power in the Belly of the Beast*, 185–223.

45. David Jacobs and Jason T. Carmichael, "Subordination and Violence Against State Control Agents: Testing Political Explanations for Lethal Assaults Against the Police," *Social Forces* 80 (June 2002): 1223–51.

46. In addressing the decline in violence in this period, historian Michael Katz credited, among other things, what he called "the management of marginalization." Katz, *Why Cities Don't Burn* (Philadelphia: University of Pennsylvania Press, 2012), 86–97.

# Index

# Acknowledgments

Many people assisted with this project. At the University of Pennsylvania, Juana Grandos made a major contribution to the research by preparing GIS maps demonstrating the correlation of murder with areas of African American settlement. Other students who provided invaluable research assistance were Julian Smyth, Samantha Napierkowski, Naomi Kaplan, Stephanie Lerner, Alison Marcus, Evan Ames, and Taryn Williams. As always, welcome support came from colleagues in Urban Studies, including particularly Elaine Simon, Michael Nairn, Mark Stern, and the indefatigable department administrator, Victoria Karkov. Members of the Urban History Seminar at Columbia University under the able direction of Lisa Keller provided many useful comments on Chapters 1 and 2 in the month after Eric's death. Among those contributing were his longtime friend and associate Camilo Jose Vergara, Robert Beauregard, and Robert Snyder, who also provided additional comments and suggestions to earlier draft material, as did Michael Fortner and Will Cooley. These comments proved especially helpful before and after Eric's death. Janet Golden and Alex and Ben Schneider read and commented on earlier drafts of the manuscript while providing unceasing care and support in the last months of Eric's life. Special thanks go to Robert Lockhart of Penn Press. He recognized the value of Eric's contribution from an early period, and he provided every encouragement necessary to move the manuscript forward throughout the process.

—*Howard Gillette Jr.*